If God Loves Me, Why Can't I Get My Locker Open?

Lorraine Peterson

BETHANY HOUSE PUBLISHERS
Minneapolis, Minnesota 55438
A Division of Bethany Fellowship, Inc.

Illustrations by LeRoy Dugan from the sketches by Neil Ahlquist.

The scripture references are taken from the Revised Standard Version of the Bible.

Published by Bethany Fellowship, Inc.
6820 Auto Club Road, Minneapolis, Minnesota 55438

Printed in the United States of America

Library of Congress Cataloging in Publication Data

Peterson, Lorraine.
   If God loves me, why can't I get my locker open?

    SUMMARY: Brief essays, Bible references, and discussion questions aid teenagers in applying Bible teachings to daily life.
    1. Youth—Prayer-books and devotions—English. [1. Prayer books and devotions] I. Title.

BV4850.P46	242'.63	80-27014

ISBN 0-87123-251-0

If God
Loves Me,
Why Can't I
Get My
Locker
Open?

About the Author

LORRAINE PETERSON was born in Red Wing, Minnesota, grew up on a farm near Ellsworth, Wisconsin, and now resides in Minneapolis. She received her B.A. (in history) from North Park College in Chicago, and has taken summer courses from the University of Minnesota and the University of Mexico in Mexico City.

Lorraine has taught high school and junior high. She has been an advisor to nondenominational Christian clubs in Minneapolis public schools and has taught teen-age Bible studies. This is her first book.

Preface

When I was twelve years old, our Bible camp speaker challenged us to start having daily devotions. I accepted that challenge. That decision to spend time with Jesus each day, in Bible study and prayer, has been one of the most important decisions I've ever made. That habit has put me in touch with the Source of all comfort and power throughout my life.

I remember the morning I received news that my mother was dying. I had read Psalm 112 the day before, and knew where to find the words, "For the righteous will never be moved. . . . He is not afraid of evil tidings; his heart is firm, trusting in the Lord." Many times the verses I've read in my regular "quiet time" contained exactly the message I needed for that day.

When I began having devotions, I had no specific guidelines to follow. In later years, whenever I would give one of my high school students a booklet of lessons for new Christians, all I could advise was, "Now, read a chapter a day in the New Testament." Inside, I knew most teens needed a more *structured* approach to Bible study, with questions to help them apply Bible truths to daily life. That's what this book is for. It is designed to make reading the Bible affect the way you clean your room and the way you respond when Dad says you can't use the car on Saturday night. I want you to discover that studying the Bible *is* exciting and relevant.*

This book was made possible because I've received so much from so many who have faithfully opened up the Bible to me: Mel Johnson and his "Tips for Teens"; Intervarsity Christian Fellowship, Campus Crusade for Christ, and the Navigators; Rev. Ernest O'Neill of Campus Church; Leighton Carlson, my Sunday school teacher; Andrew Murray, author of *New Life in Christ;* and Watchman Nee, who wrote *The Normal Christian Life.* Most of the material found in this book was first presented to the weekly Bible studies I conducted and it is to these former students who faithfully attended my Bible studies that I dedicate this book.

Many other people have also had a significant part in the development of this book. For instance, the members of the Edison High Student Life Club, who often put me to shame with their zeal and devotion to Christ, and Colleen Watson, a fellow counselor, who

---

*In order to gain the most from these lessons, keep a notebook and *write down* your answers.

made me decide to spend my summer vacation writing this book.

Finally, there are the people who supported me and helped me: Rev. and Mrs. James Kaupang who kept me on their prayer list; my father, who taught me that dreams come true only by hard work; my sister Lynn and Aunt Harriet, who insisted that I send my manuscript to a publisher; my nieces and nephews, Beth, Brett, Kaari, and Kirk, who in the earliest stages of my writing had great plans for "Aunt Lorraine's book"; and my roommates, Ruth, Karen, Vickey, and Kris, who continually helped, encouraged, and tolerated the mess.

Lorraine Peterson

Contents

How to Use This Book

To teenagers for daily devotions: In order to get the most out of these lessons, keep a notebook and *write down* the answers. The lazy part of you is saying, "I don't want to—it's too much work." However, education research supports the idea that you remember things you write down longer than things you only think about. God's Word is very important—important enough to get your best effort.

To youth workers for Sunday school or Bible study material: Leaders should assign the daily readings for the week. Ask students to write out the answers to the questions along with any new questions which they would like to discuss with the group. The leader can pick out the most important questions and ask members to contribute their findings. If it is not practical for your group to prepare in advance, it would be better to spend at least two weeks on each topic, read the material in class, and cover the questions as you go along. The teacher will want to add questions and thoughts which are specifically relevant to the particular group being taught.

Week One

THE BIGGEST DECISION OF YOUR LIFE

What Are My Choices?

When you're deciding what to do with your life, the possibilities at first seem limitless. There are hundreds of occupations to choose from and probably thousands of people you could marry. You might want to live in sunny California, frigid Alaska, or maybe even settle in Paris or Rio.

But even when you're happily married, working at your occupation, and living in your dream home, you will still have to decide what to do with your life. There are only two real choices—or at the most, three: (1) to live for yourself; (2) to live for other people—the ones you choose; (3) to live for God.

When you think of all the mistakes you've made so far, and contemplate all the errors you've watched others make, you should have a healthy fear of making your own decisions and "doing your own thing." If there is a God who showed himself to the world through His Son Jesus, and gave us the Bible, there is only ONE logical choice, and that is to live your life—all of it—for God.

"Choose this day whom ye will serve" (Josh. 24:15).

"And this is eternal life, that they know thee, the only true God, and Jesus Christ whom thou hast sent" (John 17:3).

"Thus says the Lord: 'Let not the wise man glory in his wisdom, let not the mighty man glory in his might, let not the rich man glory in his riches; but let him who glories glory in this, that he understands and knows me, that I am the Lord who practice kindness, justice, and righteousness in the earth; for in these things I delight, says the Lord' " (Jer. 9:23, 24).

1. What qualities of God can you find in these verses?
2. Why is knowing God so important?
3. What is the greatest thing you can achieve in your life?
4. Is knowing God *the most important* goal for your life? What are you doing to reach that goal?

Window Shopping—or Really Searching?

A guy named Skip loved animals and had a special interest in a pet monkey which was for sale in a local pet shop. He went to see the monkey often and enjoyed playing with it. He even dreamed about the monkey at night. Clerks who saw how much he liked the monkey kept hoping for a sale, but they always received the answer, "I don't make a lot of money. If I bought a monkey I'd have to move; my neighbors think a monkey is a weird pet. Besides, I enjoy just coming here to see him because I get the benefit of enjoying him without the responsibility of caring for him and buying his food."

Skip was a confirmed window-shopper. He refused to get involved or make a firm decision. Skip couldn't honestly say, "I went shopping today for a pet monkey, but I couldn't find one."

A lot of people are window shopping for Christianity. They are drawn by Jesus' love and the benefits of living for Christ. Because they may go to church and even read the Bible, they might be saying, "I'm seeking for God, but I just can't find Him." The truth is, if they didn't care what their friends thought, if they were willing to let God change their lives, if they would assume responsibility and if they'd consider God more important than any possession or friendship, they would find Him.

"You will seek me and find me; when you seek me with all your heart" (Jer. 29:13).

"And as he was setting out on his journey, a man ran up and knelt before him, and asked him, 'Good Teacher, what must I do to inherit eternal life?' . . . And Jesus looking upon him loved him, and said to him, 'You lack one thing; go, sell what you have, and give to the poor, and you will have treasure in heaven; and come, follow me.' At that saying his countenance fell, and he went away sorrowful; for he had great possessions" (Mark 10:17, 21, 22).

1. Was the rich man really seeking Jesus, or just window shopping? Why?
2. Notice that Jesus went straight to the point—to the thing this man wouldn't give up to follow Him. What was it?
3. What other things keep people from following Jesus?
4. If you or another person is endlessly searching for God, what is the basic reason for not finding Him?

But What If I Find It?

What are you looking for? Be careful. You'll most likely find it! You may say that you are looking for peace, or happiness, or reality, but you have probably already decided what will give you this. You may have determined that enough money will give you peace of mind—you don't want to worry about finances the way your parents do. Marrying the right person should make you "live happily ever after." Or maybe you think you can find reality if you study all the great thinkers, or take the right drugs.

If you put all your energies into trying to accumulate money, you will probably succeed at just that. If you are determined to marry a certain person, you may reach your goal. You may also become very knowledgeable about philosophy or psychology. The problem is that all of us know of people who have gotten exactly what they wanted—only to be miserable.

> Enough that God my Father knows,
> Nothing this hope can dim;
> He gives the very best to those
> Who leave the choice with Him.
> —Author unknown

"But seek first his kingdom and his righteousness, and all these things shall be yours as well" (Matt. 6:33).

"The kingdom of heaven is like treasure hidden in a field, which a man found and covered up; then in his joy he goes and sells all that he has and buys that field. Again, the kingdom of heaven is like a merchant in search of fine pearls, who, on finding one pearl of great value, went and sold all that he had and bought it" (Matt. 13:44-46).

1. How valuable was the pearl in the story Jesus told?
2. How important to you is finding God, and your place in His kingdom?
3. List the things that are hindrances to your finding God and the plan He has for you. *Be very honest and very specific.*

Is It a Real Dollar Bill, or a Counterfeit?

You've heard it and have probably said it yourself: "If that's Christianity, I don't want it." However, in many cases what the person is rejecting is not Christianity. It's Pastor Law's eighty extra commandments; it's the stubbornness displayed by some church people; or it's Matilda's hard-hearted attitude toward the girl desperately needing help. Remember that *God* decides who the real

Christians are, and that many people who claim to be Christians really aren't. However, those who are real Christians don't always live their Christianity either.

It has been said that if there weren't any real dollar bills, there wouldn't be any counterfeits. Well, there are real Christians and there are counterfeits. Don't reject Christianity because there are hypocrites in the church, because the German church didn't stand up against Hitler, or because your uncle who reads the Bible all the time yells at you. If you do reject Christianity, first take time to read the New Testament for yourself so you know what you are rejecting. Then be honest enough to admit that you're rejecting *Jesus* because you're unwilling to make the changes He requires in your life. Jesus wants to be the Boss of your life; He demands so much that many people have said of real Christianity, "If that's Christianity, I don't want it."

"Many of his disciples, when they heard it, said, 'This is a hard saying; who can listen to it?' " (John 6:60).

"After this many of his disciples drew back and no longer went about with him. Jesus said to the twelve, 'Will you also go away?' Simon Peter answered him, 'Lord, to whom shall we go? You have the words of eternal life; and we have believed, and have come to know, that you are the Holy One of God' " (John 6:66-69).

1. Why didn't Peter want to leave Jesus even if some of His teachings were tough?
2. Why does Jesus have the right to tell the disciples—and us—what to do?
3. Why do you think the other disciples left Jesus? (Reading John six could help you here.)
4. Why do people today decide not to follow Jesus?

What Makes You a Christian?

Which of these would most certainly be a Christian?
(a) Charlene Church Attender
(b) Dudley Do-Gooder
(c) Baptized Benjamin
(d) Confirmed Cynthia
(e) None of the Above

You probably answered the question correctly because you realize that just doing something outward can't change you on the inside. Yet, a lot of people think that believing the right things, using the right words, and running with the right crowd makes one a Christian. There is no magic in the words "Jesus, come into my life" if they're simply repeated because someone else thought it was a good idea.

Others think that being "born again" is just turning over a new leaf, a determination to be better. Your deciding to be different won't save you either. Of course, you have to believe that Jesus is God's Son who came to die for your sins. And, after you become a Christian you will want to do good deeds. Yet, the missing ingredient here is *repentance*. Repentance means not only feeling sorry for your sin but being willing to give it up and to turn around and face God honestly. If you admit your sin and are willing to let Jesus change you and run your life, then the words "Jesus, come into my life" have meaning, and the Spirit of Jesus miraculously enters you.

An early American evangelist was confronted on the street by a drunk. One of his critics turned to him and said, "There's one of your converts." The evangelist replied, "He must be one of mine. He certainly isn't one of God's." Are you God's convert or somebody else's?

"Repent, and believe in the gospel" (Mark 1:15).

"Jesus answered him, 'Truly, truly, I say to you, unless one is born anew, he cannot see the kingdom of God.' Nicodemus said to him, 'How can a man be born when he is old? Can he enter a second time into his mother's womb and be born?' Jesus answered, 'Truly, truly, I say to you, unless one is born of water and the Spirit, he cannot enter the kingdom of God. That which is born of the flesh is flesh, and that which is born of the Spirit is spirit. Do not marvel that I said to you, "You must be born anew" ' " (John 3:3-7).

1. With what does Jesus compare conversion? (Conversion: "accepting Christ," or being "saved")
2. Can you think of a more drastic change than being born all over again and becoming a new person?
3. According to John 3:6, can a person be called a Christian if he or she has not miraculously been changed by God on the inside? Why not?

Are You Ready to Get into the Wheelbarrow?

If I really believe something strongly enough, I will act on it. If I'm convinced that understanding chemistry will help me get through nurses' training, I'll study hard. If I'm certain that I can't make the cheerleading squad, I won't even try out. If I really believe the ice will hold, I'll go snowmobiling on the frozen lake. Saying, "I believe the ice will hold, but I'd never walk out on it," would reveal my lack of faith.

If you really believe in Jesus, you'll want to trust Him. There is an old story about a man who walked on a tightrope across Niagara Falls. Next, he wheeled an empty wheelbarrow across the rope above Niagara Falls. Then he asked his applauding crowd, "Do you believe that I can put a man in the wheelbarrow and still make it across?" Everyone shouted, "Yes!" Then he asked, "Who will get into the wheelbarrow?" No one volunteered.

Real faith will have action. Do you have "getting into the wheelbarrow" faith? This is the kind of faith needed to receive salvation.

"He who believes in the Son has eternal life; he who does not obey the Son shall not see life, but the wrath of God rests upon him" (John 3:36).

In the next passage, Paul describes what active faith meant in his life. To get the whole story, read chapters nine and twenty-six of Acts. ("Repent" means to turn around and change one's ways. "Gentiles" refers to people who are not Jewish.)

"Wherefore, O King Agrippa, I was not disobedient to the heavenly vision, but declared first to those at Damascus, then at Jerusalem and throughout all the country of Judea, and also the Gentiles, that they should repent and turn to God and perform deeds worthy of their repentance. For this reason the Jews seized me in the temple and tried to kill me" (Acts 26:19-21).

1. What did obeying God cost Paul?
2. Would it have been logical for Paul to have said to Jesus, "I have enough faith to let you save me, but not enough to do what you ask of me"? Why not?
3. When Paul preached to the people, what things did he tell them to do?
4. Is faith in Jesus real if it does not change one's life?

Will the Real Christian Please Stand Up?

When someone says, "Jesus is the Lord of my life," what picture do you conjure up in your mind—a person demanding things from Skyways Prayer Answering Service, Inc., an employee who does the King's work when conditions are favorable, or a slave who bows before his Master and calls Him "Lord"? Because we don't have slaves and absolute rulers anymore, the word "Lord" doesn't mean much to us.

Back in Roman times, calling someone Lord meant that he, like Caesar, had absolute life-and-death power over you, that he had the right to this authority, and that you would obey him. In that context, can you really say that Jesus is the Lord of your life?

In our culture, no one wants to obey. A student once remarked to me, "I think too much of myself to do as you say." If we are so self-centered that we refuse to obey Jesus, we have no right to call ourselves Christians. We can think so much of ourselves that we'll miss heaven.

"Not every one who says to me, 'Lord, Lord,' shall enter the kingdom of heaven, but he who does the will of my Father who is in heaven" (Matt. 7:21).

"But what does it say? The word is near you, on your lips and in your heart (that is, the word of faith which we preach); because, if you confess with your lips that Jesus is Lord and believe in your heart that God raised him from the dead, you will be saved. For man believes with his heart and so is justified, and he confesses with his lips and so is saved. The scripture says, 'No one who believes in him will be put to shame.' For there is no distinction between Jew and Greek; the same Lord is Lord of all and bestows his riches upon all who call upon him. For 'every one who calls upon the name of the Lord will be saved' " (Rom. 10:8-13).

1. By what actions does a person display faith in the word that is preached?
2. What promise is given in Romans 10:11? Would we need this promise if faith did not require actions?
3. What do you think confessing "Jesus is Lord" really means?
4. Can you call Jesus "Lord" and mean it?

Week Two

NO TURNING BACK

Till Death Us Do Part

If you've ever attended a traditional wedding ceremony, you've heard things like, "For better, for worse; for richer, for poorer; in sickness and in health . . . till death us do part." Taken seriously, that's a tremendous commitment to live up to. Would you describe *your* relationship with Jesus Christ as that kind of commitment, or do you think of it as "Try Jesus for ninety days; there's nothing to lose, and there's a money-back guarantee"?

Have you given yourself to Him because He is truth, because He made you, and because He who is smarter than anyone else has the right to run your life? Or do you just think it might be a good deal for you?

Do you think Jesus is pretty fortunate that you noticed Him, or do you realize that you in no way deserve His mercy and grace? The Apostle Paul referred to himself as a "slave of Jesus Christ." Do you think of Him as the Great Genie-in-the-Sky who should consider your every wish as His command?

There are *facts* you base your life on—an operation will cure appendicitis, it's safer to slow down when driving around mountain curves, and jumping from a twelfth-story window is hazardous to your health. Whether or not you feel like acting in accordance with these facts, they are valid. They are true whether or not you understand the reasons behind them, and whether or not everyone else believes in them.

You must commit yourself to Jesus because of the facts—He is "the way, the truth, and the life"—and not because He'll give you a new high. Following Jesus and His truth has great end results, but it takes a *lifetime* commitment.

"And he who does not take his cross and follow me is not worthy of me" (Matt. 10:38).

"For which of you, desiring to build a tower, does not first sit down and count the cost, whether he has enough to complete it? Otherwise, when he has laid a foundation, and is not able to finish, all who see it begin to mock him, saying, 'This man began to build and was not able to finish.' . . . . So therefore, whoever of you does not renounce all that he has cannot be my disciple" (Luke 14:28, 29, 30, 33).

1. Why is it ridiculous to start building something without finding out how much it will cost?
2. What will it cost *you* to be a real Christian?

3. Are you willing to sacrifice *everything* (popularity, wealth, comfort, dreams) in order to follow Jesus?

Receiving Jesus

The great gift of God was His Son. The great response of man is receiving Jesus. Taking Jesus into your life made you a Christian. You believed God's Word, and as an act of faith, accepted Jesus as your Savior. Because of this, God miraculously changed the direction of your life.

This is not the end of your responsibility though. Study the Bible to find out how children of God are supposed to act and what characteristics they are to have. You will notice that we are to be totally *obedient* to our Heavenly Father and totally *dependent* on Him. Even if this is not yet part of your experience, believe God's Word. Recognize that Jesus will work in you. Jesus lives within you to make you the kind of child that would bring honor to His name.

Know what God expects of you and don't try to live up to man-made rules. You don't always have to be serious, somber, and studious because Mrs. McFrown says you should be. You don't have to wear 1950 styles because Aunt Tillie thinks you'd look better if you did. But you do have to love your enemies because God says you must. How do you love your enemies when right now you hate them? This is just one of many situations in which you will have to receive Jesus and His power in order to become God's obedient child.

"But to all who received him, who believed in his name, he gave power to become children of God" (John 1:12).

"Behold, I stand at the door and knock; if any one hears my voice and opens the door, I will come in to him and eat with him, and he with me" (Rev. 3:20).

1. If we open the door to Jesus, what does He promise?
2. Jesus will come into our lives, in the first place, to save us. But Jesus may still be knocking on doors that lead to secret compartments in your life. "May I go with you on your date tonight?" "May I control your eating habits?" "Would you let me show you how to spend your money?" "Would you obey me by respecting your parents?" Are you locking Jesus out of any area of your life?
3. Eating together symbolizes fellowship, partnership, and belong-

ing to the same social class. Jesus wants to be your best Friend. He wants you to share your dreams and fears and hopes with Him, and to let Him direct you in everything. Do you have that kind of relationship with Him now?

But Don't Look in the Closet

Christ lives in your heart because you exercised faith—you let Him in. Someone has written a beautiful booklet which compares your heart to a huge house. Even after you let Jesus into your heart "house," you will discover that there are still more rooms to give to Him. Although becoming a Christian means giving Jesus your life, few people realize what that *means*. Jesus is usually invited into the "living room" and treated more like a guest than a landlord.

Little by little, Jesus shows us that He has a right to determine what goes on in the "recreation room" and to decide what is served in the "dining room." He even has the right to clean out the "closets"—to make you apologize for past words, to pay for things you've stolen, and to try to make things right with people you've wronged. He has glorious plans to remodel and redecorate your heart home— plans that are greater than you've ever dreamed of.

Most of all, Jesus wants to be your constant Companion, showing you His love continually. Let Jesus clean out your closets, make your plans, and share His life with you.

"To them God chose to make known . . . the glory of this mystery, which is Christ in you, the hope of glory" (Col. 1:27).

"And that Christ may dwell in your hearts through faith; that you, being rooted and grounded in love, may have power to comprehend with all the saints what is the breadth and length and height and depth, and to know the love of Christ which surpasses knowledge, that you may be filled with all the fullness of God" (Eph. 3:17-19).

1. How does Christ live in our hearts?
2. Love makes a house a home, and it's love that transforms your heart house. What is the Source of real love?
3. Jesus can put love in your heart that keeps on growing and that is outside the realm of human understanding. What wrong attitudes are preventing the love of Jesus from growing in you?

Your Gift to God

Have you ever tried to "ungive" a present? You don't give your mother a beautiful plant for Mother's Day and then proceed to tell her, "I'll keep it up in my room because I'll take better care of it than you will." You've been taught from the first birthday party you attended that if you give something away, you don't take it back again.

Now this also holds true for your commitment to Jesus, and it's good to renew it each day, saying, "Jesus, I have given myself to you. I will follow you and serve you—I am totally yours." If you sin after making this surrender, don't think that your surrender was insincere. It's because you are still learning how to trust Jesus and to give yourself to Him. Ask His forgiveness and reaffirm your surrender to Him.

Don't hold back anything. Confess every sin to Him. Give Him your mind and your thought life, your mouth and the words you say, as well as your heart and your love, your job, your schoolwork, your stereo, your motorcycle, and even your hairdryer. He has a right to all you are, all you do, and all you own. If you give it, Jesus will take it; and what He takes, He will care for.

I'd give you a rainbow
If I had many colors,
But alas my sky is gray.

I'd give you a lark
To greet your sunrise,
But wings were made to be free.

I'd give you a mountain,
Blue and majestic,
But all I have is one stone.

I will give you my life, Lord.
My gift to you is me.
          —Patrice Joncas

"But first they gave themselves to the Lord" (2 Cor. 8:5).

"And he said to all, 'If any man would come after me, let him deny himself and take up his cross daily and follow me. For whoever would save his life will lose it; and whoever loses his life for my sake, he will save it' " (Luke 9:23, 24).

1. Why do you actually lose your life when you approach everything with a selfish "me first" attitude?
2. Can you think of an instance in which denying yourself for the moment to obey God will not only guard you for eternal life but also protect you from trouble right here on earth?
3. Can you think of two difficult things which you might face this week if you really follow Jesus?

Lord, May I Change My Mind?

"I don't particularly feel like being a Christian today." The girl who said that expressed something most people feel at some time or another. There could be a number of reasons for this feeling. You may want to sneak out when your parents have grounded you, even though you know God commands you to obey them. Goofing around in geometry class may be more fun than doing your assignment, in spite of the fact that if Jesus physically walked into class, you'd start doing the problems. Or maybe it's a party you've been invited to; you'd like to go because all the popular kids are invited, but you know it won't be a party a Christian should attend.

Sometimes it seems so hard to be a Christian that you'd rather not try than try and fail. When you're afraid that you can't hold out as a Christian, you're forgetting that God is all powerful, and that it's not *your* ability to hold onto Him that matters, but *His* ability to hold onto you.

If you've given your life to Jesus, the Holy Spirit is at work inside you. Just as a kitten or a pine tree grows large because of the life inside, so you grow as a Christian because of the life of the Holy Spirit inside you. Choosing to sin will squelch that life inside you, but you can choose to obey. The formula for going on with Jesus is very old and very simple—"trust and obey."

"Jesus said to him, 'No one who puts his hand to the plow and looks back is fit for the kingdom of God' " (Luke 9:62).

"For God is at work in you, both to will and to work for his good pleasure" (Phil. 2:13).

"Let us know, let us press on to know the Lord; his going forth is sure as the dawn; he will come to us as the showers, as the spring rains that water the earth" (Hosea 6:3).

1. What specific area in your life will require your willingness to obey if God is going to change it?
2. What command is given in Hosea 6:3?
3. If you are really trying to obey God, how certain can you be that God will come to you?

You Can Be Sure

Back in high school I remember talking to a girlfriend about heaven. When I told her that I was certain that Jesus was in my life and that I was going to heaven, she said, "But that's presuming a lot; it sounds like a pretty proud attitude." If my status depended on my good works and flawless character, "proud" would be an understatement. But, we are saved by faith and not by works.

God does not grade on the curve. The Bible states that "you have been saved through faith . . . not because of works, lest any man should boast" (Eph. 2:8, 9). God tells us in many places in the Bible that He will forgive us and make us His children if we confess our sins and make Him the Lord of our lives. *When God says it He means it.*

There is nothing humble about calling God a liar. You don't like it when someone doubts your word; you don't want people to think that you lie. Then how can we doubt God's word? Unbelief in Jesus' power to save is nothing less than treating Him as a liar. Jesus commands us to be born again. He wouldn't command something that wasn't possible. He promised to give eternal life to anyone who believes in Him and He means it. If you completely turned your life over to Jesus, He came into your heart BECAUSE HE SAID HE WOULD.

"Truly, truly, I say to you, he who hears my word and believes him who sent me, has eternal life; he does not come into judgment, but has passed from death to life" (John 5:24).

"He who believes in the Son of God has the testimony in himself. He who does not believe God, has made him a liar, because he has not believed in the testimony that God has borne to his Son. And this is the testimony, that God gave us eternal life, and this life is in his Son. He who has the Son has life; he who has not the Son of God has not life. I write this to you who believe in the name of the Son of God, that you may know that you have eternal life" (1 John 5:10-13).

1. What is the only way you can know that you're going to heaven?
2. John wanted his readers to know that they had eternal life. How can something written 1900 years ago help *you* to have assurance of eternal life?

Assurance

The night you invited Christ into your life, you felt so clean inside and so full of joy. God seemed so near that you were sure you could never doubt Him again. But then you had to go back to "real life." There was Friday's book report, and you hadn't even picked out a book to read. As usual, every dish in the house seemed dirty the night it was your turn to do dishes, and you complained the whole time. The boss yelled at you at work, and life seemed no different from before. You heard the devil's sneering whisper, "See— you're no different. You're not really a Christian after all!" You might even have answered, "Well, I surely don't *feel* any different."

Maybe the beautiful bride feels no different after the trip to the altar either. Three days later, with a terrible sore throat and a temperature of 103° she may not *feel* one bit married. But the fact is, she *is* married. If she keep's acting on that fact, sooner or later she'll feel married.

If you truly accepted Christ, you are God's child, regardless of feeling. Trust that fact. Also remember that even if you're the weakest baby Christian, you're still a child of the King of Kings. If you stay close to Jesus, you will grow and mature in your Christian life. But if you keep doubting that you are a Christian, you'll never grow.

"Therefore, if any one is in Christ, he is a new creation; the old has passed away, behold the new has come" (2 Cor. 5:17).

"Jesus said to her, 'Your brother will rise again.' Martha said to him, 'I know that he will rise again in the resurrection at the last day.' Jesus said to her, 'I am the resurrection and the life; he who believes in me, though he die, yet shall he live, and whoever lives and believes in me shall never die. Do you believe this?' She said to him, 'Yes, Lord; I believe that you are the Christ, the Son of God, he who is coming into the world' " (John 11:23-27).

1. What promise did Jesus give Martha?
2. What did Martha believe?
3. How would Jesus have felt if Martha would have said, "I don't feel anything. You can't expect me to believe I have eternal life without giving me proof"?
4. Will you put your faith in Jesus and His work instead of in your feelings?

Week Three

THERE *IS* A DIFFERENCE!

If You Have Jesus, You Have Everything

You may have seen the greeting card showing two contented children with the caption, "If you have Jesus, you have everything." Begin each new day with that thought. You may feel like a little lost lamb in a big bad world, but Jesus, your Shepherd, is with you whether you need forgiveness, help with a problem, or someone to love you. If you fall, He'll pick you up, and when danger is near, He'll protect you. He'll help you in temptation and guide you into His perfect will.

Let Jesus be your Shepherd. Let Him be everything to you.

In Him is all I need.
In Him is all I need.

His abundance for my emptiness,
And His life for my lifelessness.

His love for my coldness,
And His light for my darkness.

His truth for my deceit,
And His joy for my sadness.

His victory for my defeat,
And His rest for my restlessness.

—Translated from the German
by Gerdi Sirtl

"He who did not spare his own Son but gave him up for us all, will he not also give us all things with him?" (Rom. 8:32).

"Though I myself have reason for confidence in the flesh also. If any other man thinks he has reason for confidence in the flesh, I have more: circumcised on the eighth day, of the people of Israel, of the tribe of Benjamin, a Hebrew born of Hebrews; as to the law a Pharisee, as to zeal a persecutor of the church, as to righteousness under the law blameless. But whatever gain I had, I counted as loss for the sake of Christ. Indeed I count everything as loss because of the surpassing worth of knowing Christ Jesus my Lord. For his sake I have suffered the loss of all things, and count them as refuse, in order that I may gain Christ" (Phil. 3:4-8).

1. What things did Paul give up in order to follow Jesus?
2. Why did Paul feel it was worth it?
3. Is there anything in your life you're holding onto because you don't trust Jesus to be everything?

Green Pastures and Still Waters

Jesus promises to give us peace. Most of us think of peace as vacationing on a Caribbean island or being able to sleep until noon on Saturday morning. Yet if peace means escape, the only way to get it is to drop out of regular day-to-day living, with its overdue library books, traffic jams, and tight schedules. Fortunately Jesus offers peace which the world can't give—peace when your mother yells at you, peace when the car runs out of gas, and peace when the band bus leaves without you—peace in the middle of pressure.

An artist once portrayed "peace" as a little bird content in a nest on the end of an oak branch sticking out over roaring Niagara Falls. *That* is peace.

There is an interesting verse in Psalms: "Blessed are the men whose strength is in thee, in whose heart are the highways to Zion" (Ps. 84:5). Zion was the hill in Jerusalem where God's temple stood. The temple was filled with the peace and presence of God. It was impossible to camp out in the temple all the time. However, since God is the Source of peace, turning our thoughts to Him makes a "highway to Zion" in our hearts.

Paul commands us to "let the peace of Christ rule" in our hearts. If you keep your mind on Jesus and you look to Him in faith, you'll find green pastures and still waters, even in the middle of the fifth-hour English class and other unexpected places.

"The Lord is my shepherd, I shall not want; he makes me lie down in green pastures. He leads me beside still waters; he restores my soul. He leads me in paths of righteousness for his name's sake. Even though I walk through the valley of the shadow of death, I fear no evil; for thou art with me; thy rod and thy staff, they comfort me. Thou preparest a table before me in the presence of my enemies; thou anointest my head with oil, my cup overflows. Surely goodness and mercy shall follow me all the days of my life; and I shall dwell in the house of the Lord for ever" (Ps. 23).

1. List ten things you shouldn't have to worry about.
2. What do "green pastures" mean for *your* life?
3. In what area of your life do you need the peace of Jesus today?

Your Best Friend—Jesus

Do you ever feel like the little kid who sings, "Nobody loves me. Everybody hates me. I'm gonna go eat worms"? If you answered "yes," join the human race. Loneliness and that "no one understands me" feeling are very common. Sometimes the people whom you think are your friends let you down. Other times they are too occupied with their own problems to notice that you need special help. Even if someone takes the time to try to help you, that person is often unable to understand your feelings.

Jesus wants to be your Friend and constant Companion, the One with whom you share your plans, your dreams, your failures, your sin, and your problems. Not only does He understand you perfectly, but He has all power, and can direct you in the right way and show you how to get out of the mess you got yourself into.

Jesus will always be your Friend—no matter what. He'll be the honest Friend who lets you know when you're doing something wrong, the comforting Friend to whom you can pour out your heart, and the Counselor who will help you make your future plans.

Good friends spend a lot of time together. Jesus can't help you if you don't talk to Him, and He can't advise you if you don't listen to Him. You need a Friend like Jesus. Take the time to get to know Him.

"No longer do I call you servants, for the servant does not know what his master is doing; but I have called you friends, for all that I have heard from my Father I have made known to you" (John 15:15).

"For he hath said, 'I will never leave thee, nor forsake thee' " (Heb. 13:5, KJV).

"Fear not, for I am with you, be not dismayed, for I am your God; I will strengthen you, I will help you, I will uphold you with my victorious right hand" (Isa. 41:10).

"No man shall be able to stand before you all the days of your life; as I was with Moses, so I will be with you; I will not fail you or forsake you" (Josh. 1:5).

1. How do we know that Jesus is always with us?
2. Because Jesus is always with us, what commands are we given?
3. During the next week, what should you do differently because you know Jesus is your friend?

Happiness Is Jesus

Do you want to be happy? You might respond, "That's a dumb question. Of course, *everyone* wants to be happy."

God loves you and wants to give you real joy, but like everything God has for us, it must be on *His* terms, not ours. If you're looking for gladness, you won't find it, because you're looking for a feeling, for something within yourself. Look to Jesus, follow Jesus, believe in Jesus, and joy becomes automatic. Gladness is only proof that something really satisfies you. Does your happiness come from the fact that Jesus really satisfies you and that you enjoy doing His will?

In the Bible, light and joy usually go together. You can even see a glow on the face of a person who is genuinely happy. When gloom descends it's because of one of these reasons: (1) ignorance of all God can do; (2) doubt that God can work in a tough situation; (3) unwillingness to give up everything to Jesus; (4) sin.

God can give you joy and light in the middle of absolutely terrible circumstances; there are Christians around who prove it by their lives. I'll never forget Helen. I met her once when I was eighteen. Helen was a hunch-back lady, caring for her dying mother in a rickety old house on an out-of-the-way farm. She had never been able to realize her dream of attending a Bible school, and now found herself in a very lonely and difficult situation. Helen's face was beaming and she talked constantly of the Lord and His many blessings. She knew that if she had Jesus, it was possible for her to find all her happiness in Him.

Jesus assured us that whoever follows Him "shall not walk in darkness." Deep-down joy doesn't necessarily mean absence of pain and heartache. Only hopelessness causes depression—but the Christian can always have hope and faith in any situation because God is all-powerful.

"The joy of the Lord is your strength" (Neh. 8:10).

"And he said to them, 'Did you receive the Holy Spirit when you believed?' And they said, 'No, we have never even heard that there is a Holy Spirit' " (Acts 19:2).

"And he did not do many mighty works there, because of their unbelief" (Matt. 13:58).

"If you keep my commandments, you will abide in my love, just as I have kept my Father's commandments and abide in his love. These things I have spoken to you, that my joy may be in you, and that your joy may be full" (John 15:10, 11).

1. What are some reasons for Christians not experiencing joy?
2. Which of these reasons do you feel is your biggest problem at the moment? Ask God to show you what to do about it.

This Job Takes Jesus

A six-year-old boy was terrified to walk past the house of a big bully. This bully would always beat him up. Then one day the boy's fifteen-year-old brother walked with him past the house. The bully never even appeared.

The six-year-old was safe as long as he was accompanied by his brother. But one day he became overconfident and decided to go past the home of the big bully all by himself. He was badly beaten up. At first he was afraid to tell his big brother, but when he did, the big brother taught the bully a lesson. He also instructed his little brother never to walk by that house alone again.

Jesus intends that we have victory over sin—not once in a while, but constantly. If we approach life in our own strength, sin will defeat us just as the bully beat up the child. However, Jesus within us is all-powerful and He has never yet lost a fight with the devil.

Stay close to Jesus and be afraid to venture into anything without His presence and approval. Bring every sin to Him. Never try to deal with it yourself. It is as ridiculous for you to try to deal with sin by yourself as it is for a beaten-up six-year-old to take on a big bully. Jesus will forgive you and give you strength for the next time. Jesus is a Savior from sin. You don't overcome sin with a little help from Jesus, but when Jesus himself lives within you, He can insure victory over sin.

"And you shall call his name Jesus, for he will save his people from their sins" (Matt. 1:21).

"I confess my iniquity, I am sorry for my sin" (Ps. 38:18).

"I can do all things in him who strengthens me" (Phil. 4:13).

1. Why is it sometimes difficult to confess sin?
2. Why is it necessary to confess sin?
3. Once your sin is confessed and forgiven, what can Jesus do through you?
4. Reread Philippians 4:13 several times, replacing "all things" with something specific in your life. For example, "I can study for the geometry test through Christ who strengthens me."

Are There Any Goliaths in Your Life?

Breaking that date for Friday night, saying "no" to drugs, starting the homework that's due on Friday, or replacing the stolen bike sometimes can seem like beady-eyed nine-foot-high giants. Life is full of Goliaths. Jesus is the One with the power to win the victory over each of them, and He wants to give that power to us.

The story is told of a mother who visited her son's dormitory room at college. She was disappointed to see the walls filled with immoral pictures. She said nothing but mailed her son a present—a beautifully framed picture of Christ. He put it on the wall, and as he looked at it, he thought of Jesus. He was forced to take down the other pictures. The power of Jesus is like that—it wins over wrong thinking and sinful actions.

The power of Jesus is not just for facing emergencies and full-grown Goliaths. Do you realize that Goliath was once a cute, helpless little baby? The most innocent or potentially worthwhile thing can become a monster unless it is under the control and guidance of Jesus. Even a search for love can turn into a horrible experience if Jesus is not in charge of it.

Take all your plans, all your decisions, and all your temptations to Jesus. Let Jesus fight the Goliaths in your life.

"And Jesus came and said to them, 'All authority in heaven and on earth has been given to me' " (Matt. 28:18).

"Then David said to the Philistine, 'You come to me with a sword and with a spear and with a javelin; but I come to you in the name of the Lord of hosts, the God of the armies of Israel, whom you have defied. This day the Lord will deliver you into my hand. . . .' And David put his hand in his bag and took out a stone, and slung it, and struck the Philistine on his forehead; the stone sank into his forehead, and he fell on his face to the ground" (1 Sam. 17:45, 46, 49).

1. Why do you think David won his fight with Goliath?
2. What are the giants in your life right now? Are you facing them the way David faced Goliath?
3. What might have been the ending of this story if David had trusted in his own strength?

I Am Weak but He Is Strong

Jesus wants to be your strength, but He can't be unless you let Him. In order to let Jesus be your strength, you must be weak—by God's definition; you must recognize that you are unable to live the Christian life—period. It is not a matter of desperately trying to be kind to a crabby boss and getting a little help from Jesus to push you over the top. It is not witnessing like mad in your own strength and getting a snitch of God's power to keep going. No, it's recognizing that Jesus meant it when He said, "Apart from me you can do nothing" (John 15:5).

Sometimes, we use the word "weakness" to cover up sins. A little child who comes in from playing doesn't usually get by with saying, "I'm too weak to clean my room." Spending little time in Bible study and not helping others is not due to "weakness." It's more accurate to say, "I'm too lazy," or, "I think other things are more important."

A child who struggles to put his shoe on the wrong foot, disregarding his mother's instruction, is not weak. He is *disobedient*. You may be trying to do something God doesn't want you to do; you can't expect His strength for that. If your mother baked a birthday cake for your younger sister, asking you not to touch it, your eating three pieces before the party is not weakness; it is pure selfishness.

If you want God's strength, you can have it. First of all, stop calling sin "laziness" and disobedience "weakness." Second, recognize that you don't just need *some* help from Jesus—you need Him to do the whole thing, from beginning to end. Now, this does not mean sitting in a chair for the next twenty years until a voice from heaven tells you to stand up. It does mean recognizing that you can't drive a car, wash the dishes, take a test, or call your girlfriend *in such a way as to glorify and honor God* unless you admit your complete dependence on Him. Of course you can physically accomplish any of these things. It's *pleasing God* that you cannot do on your own. Just as you would constantly seek the guidance of your teacher while performing an experiment with explosives, so you should realize that the relationships and responsibilities of life require God's supervision if they are not to blow up in your face.

Once you acknowledge your weakness, by faith claim God's strength. God promises strength for the weak. He has enough strength no matter what you're facing, as long as you don't rely on your own resources. Andrew Murray puts it this way, "The Christian is strong in His Lord—not sometimes strong and sometimes weak, but always weak and therefore always strong."

"My grace is sufficient for you, for my power is made perfect in weakness" (2 Cor. 12:9).

"But Peter said, 'I have no silver and gold, but I give you what I have; in the name of Jesus Christ of Nazareth, walk.' And he took him by the right hand and raised him up; and immediately his feet and ankles were made strong. And leaping up he stood and walked and entered the temple with them, walking and leaping and praising God" (Acts 3:6-8).

1. What did *Jesus* do for the lame man?
2. What sin in your life have you been excusing as "weakness"? Confess it to the Lord as sin and begin to obey God in that area.
3. For what do you need the strength of Jesus today? Ask Him for it.

Week Four

HOW TO WIN THE WAR AGAINST SIN

When It's Legal to Hate

Do you *hate* sin? God does. You might hear someone say, "Why does God let little children starve and suffer?" However, the real culprit is sin. It was greed that started the war, alcoholism that misspent the money, and uncontrolled anger that caused the beating. A heresy of our day teaches that finally even the devil will go to heaven! The devil is the author of sin and delights in seeing starving children, broken homes, and misunderstood teenagers. You should hate the devil and hate sin.

Sin hurts God and makes people unhappy. If you are to talk to God at all, the first thing you must bring to Him is your sin. You had to confess your sin and bring it to Jesus in order to become a Christian. As a child of God, confession of sin is one of your greatest privileges. God's holiness actually eradicates sin. His holiness is like fire that consumes evil, or a spot remover that erases every stain.

Our first tendency is to cover sin or to try to lessen its impact. Have you noticed that the kid who cheated on the test goes out of his way to be nice to the teacher? If you stay out past the time you promised you'd be in, isn't it easier to do the dishes for your mother than to tell her the truth? But sin is so terrible that you can't cover it, patch it up, or rework it. It's like rotting garbage. The only thing to do with it is throw it away. But you can never get rid of your sin unless you are completely honest with God and with people you have wronged.

"He who conceals his transgressions [sins] will not prosper, but he who confesses and forsakes them will find mercy" (Prov. 28:13).

"When I declared not my sin, my body wasted away through my groaning all day long. For day and night thy hand was heavy upon me; my strength was dried up as by the heat of summer. I acknowledged my sin to thee, and I did not hide my iniquity; I said, 'I will confess my transgressions to the Lord'; then thou didst forgive the guilt of my sin" (Ps. 32:3-5).

1. What are the symptoms of a person who is trying to cover up unconfessed sin?
2. Just as pain tells you to pull your hand off the hot stove, guilt reveals the sin you must get rid of. If a person refused to take his or her hand off the hot stove and yet kept complaining about the pain, no one would be very sympathetic. Somehow, though, we

will do everything with our guilt feelings except confess our sin. Confess any covered-up sins to God—and to people you've wronged. Then accept God's forgiveness and refuse to entertain more guilt.

Does This Shake You Up a Little?

Do you know what God thinks about "little white lies"? A "little white lie" is a dangerous sin which can break your communication with God and damage your relations with other people. The Bible tells the story of Ananias and Sapphira, a nice Jerusalem couple who sold their land and gave the money to the church. Now that's a very generous thing to do. There was just one problem—they pretended to give all of the money, when they really gave only part of it. When Ananias told this "little white lie," Peter answered, "You have not lied to men but to God." When Ananias heard these words, he dropped dead. That is probably the reason why Noah and the ark is a much more popular Bible story!

Maybe you'd better look at your own life. Do you lie to give false impressions? Do you exaggerate to make people listen to your stories? Do you hint that you are a better ball player than you really are? Would your comments lead others to think that you had more dates than a palm tree? Confess these lies to God. Remember that He loves you exactly the way you are, and it isn't necessary to give a false impression to Him, or anyone. Also ask Him to help you overcome any bragging habits you have established. Never justify your "little white lies." Confess them as sin and determine to tell the truth.

"Be sure your sin will find you out" (Num. 32:23).

"After an interval of about three hours his wife came, not knowing what had happened. And Peter said to her, 'Tell me whether you sold the land for so much.' And she said, 'Yes, for so much.' But Peter said to her, 'How is it that you have agreed together to tempt the Spirit of the Lord? Hark, the feet of those that have buried your husband are at the door, and they will carry you out.' Immediately she fell down at his feet and died. When the young men came in they found her dead, and they carried her out and buried her beside her husband. And great fear came upon the whole church, and upon all who heard of these things" (Acts 5:7-11).

1. How do we know that Ananias and Sapphira were guilty of "premeditated lying"?
2. Do you ever find it easier to go along with something that is not completely honest because another Christian suggests it?
3. Do you have a real fear of saying or doing something that is not entirely honest?

Even If They Stone You

The Scarlet Letter, not a popular book nowadays, is an early American novel in Puritan Massachusetts. In the story a young minister fathers an illegitimate child. He is suspected by no one and the mother will not disclose his identity. The young minister says from the pulpit that he is the worst of sinners; he constantly condemns himself. At the same time, he refuses to do the one necessary thing—make a direct confession of his specific sin before God and the people, with the intention of facing the consequences. Because he refused to do this, he was most miserable. Finally, his approaching death made him confess publicly, but he had no time to enjoy his clear conscience.

Actually, it would be better to say nothing than to repeat, "and Jesus, forgive all my sins," every night for five years. It's better to tell God that you have nothing to confess than to confess just for the sake of confessing. Ask the Holy Spirit to point out specific sin in your life. Confess that sin to God—and to another person if you have wronged him or her.

Whenever you feel guilty, ask the Holy Spirit to show you if you've done something specifically wrong. Ask with an attitude of willingness to face God honestly. If God doesn't show you anything, then dismiss the guilty feeling. That "yucky" worthless feeling, which is vague and uncertain, comes from the devil. Ignore it and forget it. However, the conviction of specific sin is from the Holy Spirit and must be dealt with immediately.

"Against thee, thee only, have I sinned, and done that which is evil in thy sight, so that thou art justified in thy sentence and blameless in thy judgment" (Ps. 51:4).

"And Achan answered Joshua, 'Of a truth I have sinned against the Lord God of Israel, and this is what I did: when I saw among the spoil a beautiful mantle from Shinar, and two hundred shekels of silver, and a bar of gold weighing fifty shekels, then I coveted them and took them; and behold, they are hidden in the earth inside my tent. . . .' And all Israel stoned him with stones" (Josh. 7:20, 21, 25).

1. Notice how specific Achan's confession of his sin was. How do you think he felt after he confessed?
2. Are your confessions of sin specific or general?
3. God could not bless Israel again until Achan's sin was dealt with. In view of that, and in view of the eternal consequences of sin, was Achan's confession worth it, even if it sealed his death?

But . . .

Are you able to talk yourself into and out of almost anything? Can you think of sixty-nine good reasons for not doing your history lesson? Are you able to defend yourself for ten minutes straight when your mother mentions that a bulldozer may be needed to get your room cleaned out? Can you rationalize that running with a rowdy group of friends won't hurt you?

If you decide to prove that everything you do is okay, you will hurt yourself immeasurably. People who are really good at rationalizing won't take advice—but it's amazing what you can learn from other people *if you listen.*

Jesus demanded a "no ifs, ands, or buts" obedience from His disciples. If you keep making excuses, you won't obey your parents, your teachers, or God. Probably the worst thing about an excuse-maker is that he or she can't really ask God for forgiveness. If you can't admit that you're dead wrong and that you need forgiveness, God won't forgive you. Your confession can't be, "God, if you had to live with my sister, you'd blow your stack too—and besides, she started it. By the way, I'd like forgiveness for getting angry." God wants you to deal directly and honestly with your sin. No excuses are allowed.

"For he flatters himself in his own eyes that his iniquity [sin] cannot be found out and hated" (Ps. 36:2).

"But he said to him, 'A man once gave a great banquet, and invited many; and at the time for the banquet he sent his servant to say to those who had been invited, "Come; for all is now ready." But they all alike began to make excuses. The first said to him, "I have bought a field, and I must go out and see it; I pray you, have me excused." And another said, "I have bought five yoke of oxen, and I go to examine them; I pray you, have me excused." And an-

other said, "I have married a wife, and therefore I cannot come" ' "
(Luke 14:16-20).

1. Since oxen and fields can wait, and women love to go out to eat, what were these excuse-makers really saying?
2. Jesus is asking you to follow Him completely and to be frank and honest about your sin. What excuses do you have for not obeying?
3. Why do excuses keep you from seeing yourself as you really are?
4. What is the real motive behind the excuses you are giving God for your disobedience to God? Talk this over with Him, asking Him to help you stop making excuses.

Eve Made Me Do It

I walked into the principal's office just in time to hear a good-looking blond boy's, "But he started it!" cut off by the principal's booming voice: "I don't care what the other guy did. I want to know what *you* did." Just as the student had to face the principal because of *his own* actions, each of us must face God, knowing that we are responsible for our own deeds; we can't blame anybody else.

My father tells about the first lie he ever heard my sister tell. "Chickie did it. Don't spank me." She was barely two. No one has to teach us to cover up for our mistakes and sins. That comes naturally. If we don't stop blaming other people, we will never build an honest and healthy relationship with God. It doesn't matter if it is ninety-five percent the fault of the other person. God expects us to confess our part to Him and to apologize to the other person—and not in such a way as to force an apology in return.

We are not responsible for making other people confess their sins. We are only responsible for ourselves. One of the devil's best tricks to keep us from having pure hearts is getting us to concentrate on the faults and sins of others. If God had a loudspeaker in the sky to give us constant audible advice, I think we'd often hear, "MIND YOUR OWN BUSINESS." Confess your sin without blaming anyone but yourself.

"When Peter saw him, he said to Jesus, 'Lord, what about this man?' Jesus said to him, 'If it is my will that he remain until I come, what is that to you? Follow me!' " (John 21:21, 22).

"Who are you to pass judgment on the servant of another? It is before his own master that he stands or falls. And he will be upheld, for the Master is able to make him stand" (Rom. 14:4).

"The soul that sins shall die. The son shall not suffer for the iniquity [sin] of the father, nor the father suffer for the iniquity of the son; the righteousness of the righteous shall be upon himself, and the wickedness of the wicked shall be upon himself" (Ezek. 18:20).

1. Why is it so easy to blame others for our own failures?
2. Why do we find it easier to excuse ourselves for wrongdoing than to excuse others?
3. If you have been blaming your parents, your church, your school, or your friends for the way you act, talk to God about your attitude. Do exactly what He tells you to do.

Do You Enjoy Being Kidnapped?

Not long ago, the newspapers carried the story of a wealthy Italian girl who was kidnapped. Her parents came up with the ransom money, only to find that she liked living with her kidnapper! She refused to be freed.

Do you enjoy your sin? Do you find self-pity comforting? Do you appreciate the way your temper helps you get your own way? Do you find that dwelling on unclean thoughts is an enjoyable pastime? If you answered "yes," you'd have to admit that confession of these sins wouldn't be completely sincere. Real confession implies willingness to stop sinning—willingness to hate the sin you're confessing. You still might fall sometimes. However, there is a great difference between trying to go through every red light without getting caught and determining never to go through a red light again, though unconsciously breaking the law a few times.

Treat even the thought of sin like a traffic light which has turned red—stop before you get into it. If you have decided always to stop at red lights, your conscious decision soon becomes subconscious, and obeying traffic lights becomes easier and easier. Set your mind completely against sin. Be willing to take any action necessary to follow God. Don't just confess sin. Determine to stop doing it.

"And put on the new nature, created after the likeness of God in true righteousness and holiness" (Eph. 4:24).

"When you spread forth your hands, I will hide my eyes from you; even though you make many prayers, I will not listen; your hands are full of blood. Wash yourselves; make yourselves clean; remove the evil of your doings from before my eyes; cease to do evil, learn to do good; seek justice, correct oppression; defend the fatherless, plead for the widow. Come now, let us reason together, says the Lord: though your sins are like scarlet, they shall be as white as snow; though they are red like crimson, they shall become like wool" (Isa. 1:15-18).

1. Why wouldn't God listen to the prayers of His people, according to Isaiah 1?
2. Is there any reason why God won't listen to your prayers?
3. God wants you not only to stop doing wrong, but also to "learn to do good." What kind of student are you when it comes to learning to do right?

Repent? You've Got To Be Kidding!

I'll never forget it. At a senior high Bible camp, as we silently sat around the campfire, God's power became very real, and His Holy Spirit began convicting people of sin. A seventeen-year-old boy who had been one of the troublemakers started sobbing and saying, "I'm a terrible sinner," "I'm a terrible sinner." That night kids not only confessed sin, they also genuinely repented.

Repentance means turning around and going in the opposite direction. Those kids were serious about giving their lives to God. Dates were cancelled so campers could go back to their cabins to pray and apologize for wrong things they had said or done. The next day camp seemed a little bit like heaven. The whole atmosphere had changed.

Repentance always includes these things: (1) A deep sense of sinfulness and a realization that a holy God can't look upon our sin. A flippant "All have sinned so I'm a sinner too—big deal" won't make it. We must recognize the seriousness of sin. (2) A desire to get rid of our sin badly enough to obey God—to do whatever He says must be done. (3) A determination to live our lives for Jesus and not for ourselves. There must be a *complete change of direction*.

You may not hear the word "repent" very often, but if you don't experience the ingredients of repentance, you'll never have a solid relationship with God.

"I tell you, No; but unless you repent you will all likewise perish" (Luke 13:3).

"Many also of those who were now believers came, confessing and divulging their practices. And a number of those who practiced magic arts brought their books together and burned them in the sight of all; and they counted the value of them and found it came to fifty thousand pieces of silver. So the word of the Lord grew and prevailed mightily" (Acts 19:18-20).

1. How do you know that those people in Acts really meant it when they confessed their sin?

2. Do you have a book that needs to be thrown away, a "bridge" to burn, or a friendship you must terminate?
3. From Acts 19:20, what is the result when people confess and then follow through with *action*?

Week Five

THAT NASTY STUFF CALLED "SIN"

Sin and Separation

Do you remember doing things such as avoiding Mr. Farnsworth for years because you hit a baseball through his window when he was vacationing in Colorado? Or trying to keep your mother from discovering that you had broken her most beautiful vase? Or hoping you wouldn't meet the kid whose bike you stole? If you've ever done anything like that—and most of us have—you know how uncomfortable the person you have wronged can make you feel, and even if that person knows nothing about what you have done.

Sin makes us feel very uncomfortable around God, and there is no way we can hide what we have done from Him. YOU CAN NEVER GROW AS A CHRISTIAN WITH UNCONFESSED SIN IN YOUR LIFE. It doesn't matter if it is something you did yesterday, or whether it happened five years ago. To feel close to God again, you must clear up your sin.

If you think back on your life again, you may also be able to recall confessing what you did and finding a beautiful relationship with another person completely restored. When I was a child, my mother left an open can of red paint on the kitchen floor while she went out into the yard. While she was gone, my sister and I were running through the kitchen and dumped the whole thing over. We ran out to tell my mother what had happened. She not only forgave us, but said, "When you do something wrong, always tell me right away. Because you told me immediately, I can clean up the floor without permanent damage. If you had tried to hide it, the kitchen floor would have been red for years."

When you do something wrong, remember the can of red paint. If you don't confess it immediately, it will do more harm and will be much harder to confess later. If you have something from your past that must be made right, clear it up immediately before it gets worse.

"If I had cherished iniquity [sin] in my heart, the Lord would not have listened" (Ps. 66:18).

"Behold, the Lord's hand is not shortened, that it cannot save, or his ear dull, that it cannot hear; but your iniquities have made a separation between you and your God, and your sins have hid his face from you so that he does not hear" (Isa. 59:1, 2).

1. If you feel like avoiding Bible study, church services, and youth leaders, what could be the reason?

2. Is there specific sin in your life that is separating you from God? What is it?

Hiding in the Garden Is Not Advised

The story of Adam and Eve is so familiar that we forget we can learn something from it. We could title their experience, "All the Wrong Ways to Handle Any Situation." Adam and Eve did all the dumbest things. The sad part is that their actions have been repeated millions of times.

Eve listened to the devil as he questioned God. That is very dangerous because we are then assuming that we know more than God, and have the right to revise His commandments. Eve hadn't listened to God carefully enough to be sure about what He had actually said. She inaccurately repeated His instructions.

Next, Eve believed the devil's lies. What he said seemed logical so she bought it. Remember that your logic is never better than God's.

Eve then desired the forbidden fruit. I've heard a mother say to her child, "You can't have it, but it's okay to want it." That is not true when it comes to temptation. If the devil can make you dwell on your desire to have something that's wrong, he has won half his battle.

Misery and sin like company. Eve not only sinned but convinced Adam to join in her sin. Then instead of confessing, they made silly fig-leaf outfits and played the first game of hide-and-seek! To say the least, God was not impressed.

Anything you do to try to hide your sin is just as ridiculous. You don't have to repeat the garden-of-Eden experiment. The results are always the same.

"Then desire when it has conceived gives birth to sin; and sin when it is full grown brings forth death" (James 1:15).

"So when the woman saw that the tree was good for food, and that it was a delight to the eyes, and that the tree was to be desired to make one wise, she took of its fruit and ate; and she also gave some to her husband, and he ate. Then the eyes of both were opened, and they knew that they were naked; and they sewed fig leaves together and made themselves aprons. And they heard the sound of the Lord God walking in the garden in the cool of the day, and the man and his wife hid themselves from the presence of the Lord God among the trees of the garden" (Gen. 3:6-8).

1. What attitude did Adam and Eve have toward God after their sin?
2. How will sin affect your relationship with God?
3. In what ways have you tried to hide from God when you have sinned?

The Blood of Jesus

If your kidneys failed to function, the only way that you could hope to again live a normal, healthy life would be by receiving a kidney transplant. If I volunteered to donate my kidney to you, you would really owe me your life. If you honestly asked me what you could do to repay me and I told you to give me your antique ring, you'd be obligated to do exactly as I said. To me, that ring would be the most valuable thing you could give me.

Have you ever wondered how the blood of Jesus can take away our sins? Has the idea of sacrificing animals in the Old Testament, to cover sin until Jesus died, been a terribly difficult concept for you to understand? Blood is valuable to God because He says it is. God created the world and He made the rules. We couldn't live without blood running through our veins; to give His blood for us, Jesus had to die, showing how terrible sin is and how much it cost God to forgive us.

Yet, there is no completely logical way to figure out why blood is valuable to God, so we must accept it by faith. Human logic would say that we should try to do enough good deeds to outweigh the bad ones. God says, "No." Man's idea is to show penitence and remorse to try and make God feel sorry for us. But that isn't necessary. Jesus already shed His blood for our sins. You can't do a thing to make yourself acceptable in God's sight. Only Jesus' blood can remove your sin. That is what is valuable to God.

"But if we walk in the light, as he is in the light, we have fellowship with one another, and the blood of Jesus his Son cleanses us from all sin" (1 John 1:7).

"Indeed, under the law almost everything is purified with blood,

and without the shedding of blood there is no forgiveness of sins"
(Heb. 9:22).

"For this is my blood of the covenant [promise], which is poured
out for many for the forgiveness of sins" (Matt. 26:28).

1. What is God's requirement for the forgiveness of sins?
2. Do you really believe Jesus' blood is what takes away your sins,
   or do you try to feel bad, or do more good works to "make up" for
   what you've done?
3. Because Jesus gave His blood—His life—for you, what is the
   only logical thing you can give Him in return?

So Satan Is Accusing You Again!

Do you hear the devil whispering discouraging things to
you? He'll suggest things like, "God never forgave you—look how
bad you are"; "You're a failure and you might as well stop even
trying to be a Christian"; "Don't bother trying to confess that
sin. God won't even want to talk to you after this."

Obviously, if we have done something wrong and refuse to be
honest and confess it, we should feel guilty—because we are. But
I'm talking about that vague feeling of failure and discourage-
ment, or the constant rehashing of old sins you've confessed before. The devil loves to accuse Christians, and he spends twenty-
four hours a day doing it. The reason we have so much trouble is
that we fall for his tricks.

The devil might say, "You're a rotten Christian. You didn't
feel one bit like helping that crabby neighbor, Mrs. Jones, carry
in her groceries yesterday—and Christians are supposed to love
to help everybody." Our usual reply is something like, "Well, I
did mow the lawn without my mother saying a word—so there."
Other times we answer, "You're right. I'm a terrible, awful, lousy
Christian who should flee the planet."

In both cases, we are trying to find righteousness and goodness within ourselves, and the Bible teaches that it just isn't
there. The right answer for you to give is, "Big deal, Satan. I've
confessed that, and it's Jesus' blood which takes away my sin
and clears my conscience. I don't expect to find something good
inside me because it just isn't there. But Jesus has forgiven me. I
never need to think of that sin again. Besides, you were defeated
by Jesus on the cross and will be completely destroyed at the end
of the world."

"When he [the devil] lies, he speaks according to his own nature, for he is a liar and the father of lies" (John 8:44).

"And the great dragon was thrown down, that ancient serpent, who is called the Devil and Satan, the deceiver of the whole world—he was thrown down to the earth, and his angels were thrown down with him. And I heard a loud voice in heaven, saying, "Now the salvation and the power and the kingdom of our God and the authority of his Christ have come, for the accuser of our brethren has been thrown down, who accused them day and night before our God. And they have conquered him by the blood of the Lamb and by the word of their testimony, for they loved not their lives unto death' " (Rev. 12:9-11).

1. What kinds of things does the devil do to discourage you?
2. According to Revelation 12, how can the devil be conquered?

But God Is on My Side

When you have a hassle or a problem, it's nice to have someone stick up for you. The devil is always trying to condemn you. The comments of non-Christians are part of his ammunition: "After all, what can one expect of a religious fanatic." "I thought you were a Christian," or, "But then, everyone from your church is weird."

When you deliberately do wrong, you open the door for the devil because he then has a definite reason to accuse you. Of course, he won't stop with the true accusation. He'll bring up some false ones also to completely wipe you out. As soon as you confess your sin to God and claim Jesus' blood, you can effectively resist the devil's accusations. Pray honestly, and if God doesn't reveal any specific sin, ignore Satan's whispers. Then remember that *God is on your side*. He loves you, He forgives you, and He sent Jesus to die for you.

You are working for God, not the devil. You would think it strange if the manager of Burger King came over to MacDonald's to tell one of the employees that he was making the French fries wrong. He would have no right to criticize the employee of another company. God is the only One who has the right to criticize you. If you are doing God's will, Satan's whispers and the comments of other people should not disturb you. God is your Boss. Serve Him faithfully and listen carefully to His correction, always keeping in mind that *He is on your side*.

"With the Lord on my side I do not fear. What can man do to me?" (Ps. 118:6).

"What then shall we say to this? If God is for us, who is against us? He who did not spare his own Son but gave him up for us all, will he not also give us all things with him? Who shall bring any charge against God's elect? It is God who justifies; who is to condemn? Is it Christ Jesus, who died, yes, who was raised from the dead, who is at the right hand of God, who indeed intercedes [prays] for us?" (Rom. 8:31-34).

1. Why is God for us?
2. God has elected us, or chosen us, because He loves us. Who is the only one who has the right to bring a charge against us or to condemn us?
3. Let God convict you of specific sin and confess it. Why is it wrong to accept the devil's condemning words?

How Did I Become a Sinner?

Does sinning make you a sinner, or do you sin because you're a sinner? None of us likes anger, jealousy, hatred, lying, or selfishness, and we are quite willing to admit that they are bad. Nevertheless, we tend to think of ourselves as good people who get angry only when we have a right to, who hate only people everybody else would hate, and who lie only when we get into especially tough circumstances. Yet, if you go on a "I'm-going-to-be-good" campaign, you'll find that something inside you just wants to be bad. Benjamin Franklin tried to eliminate some bad traits by spending a week overcoming each. He was surprised that his experiment failed.

The moment you first willfully disobeyed God, you became a sinner. You are a student because you study, a person is a farmer because he farms, you are a sinner because you sin.

There are a lot of inherited things about you that you can't help—freckles, curly hair, a long nose—but not sin. You were born with imperfect judgment and independent emotions, which don't help the situation, but you *chose* to sin—just like every other person on this planet.

"We have turned every one to his own way" (Isa. 53:6). That is why, in yourself, you can't obey God. You're like a train that has headed itself down the wrong track; the only way it can go the right way is for someone to pick it up and set it on the right track.

If you'll give Jesus control of your life, He can put you "on track" to live in victory.

"As it is written: 'None is righteous [good], no, not one' " (Rom. 3:10).

"And you he made alive, when you were dead through the trespasses and sins in which you once walked, following the course of this world, following the prince of the power of the air, the spirit that is now at work in the sons of disobedience. Among these we all once lived in the passions of our flesh, following the desires of body and mind, and so we were by nature children of wrath like the rest of mankind. But God, who is rich in mercy, out of the great love with which he loved us, even when we were dead through our trespasses, made us alive together with Christ (by grace you have been saved)" (Eph. 2:1-5).

1. What are the characteristics of a person who is following "the course of this world"?
2. How does Christ change our sinful natures and make us new people?

Whose Slave Are You?

Watching "Roots" on TV, or studying United States history can make you hate slavery. In fact, maybe you couldn't imagine anything worse than being a slave. But did you know that millions of people are slaves today? *Their master is sin, and sin is a terrible master.* It binds people until they are unable to make choices or see truth.

I remember an object lesson I saw as a child. A visiting pastor picked out one boy from the audience and tied the boy's arms together with a strand of thread. It was easy for the boy to break the thread. Winding the thread around three times made it a little harder to break. Finally, so many threads bound the boy's arms together that he could do nothing. "Sin," the pastor explained to us, "is like that thread. It looks so harmless at first, but it takes away your freedom and makes you a prisoner."

If you know an alcoholic, a drug addict, or a very bitter person, you have seen this principle at work. The only way to break away from sin is to get a new master—Jesus Christ. If you obey Jesus, He gives you power to overcome sin. But you can't be your own master and stay in the "middle of the road." You must either be a slave of sin or a slave of Christ. Whose slave are you?

"No one can serve two masters; for either he will hate the one and love the other, or he will be devoted to the one and despise the other. You cannot serve God and mammon [the false god of riches]" (Matt. 6:24).

"Let not sin therefore reign in your mortal bodies, to make you obey their passions. Do not yield your members to sin as instruments of wickedness, but yield yourselves to God as men who have been brought from death to life, and your members to God as instruments of righteousness. For sin will have no dominion over you, since you are not under law but under grace. What then? Are we to sin because we are not under law but under grace? By no means! Do you not know that if you yield yourselves to any one as obedient slaves, you are slaves of the one whom you obey, either of sin, which leads to death, or of obedience, which leads to righteousness?'' (Rom. 6:12-16).

1. Why can't you successfully serve God and follow the devil at the same time?
2. What are the advantages of being an obedient slave of Jesus Christ?
3. Judging by how you've lived your life in the last week, whose slave are you?

Week Six

FORGIVENESS

Sin Removal

Do you live as if you are *completely* forgiven? Or do you let the devil whisper things to you like, "You can't expect to live a holy life because a person with a past like yours will never be able to reform," or, "What you've done is so terrible that God will never be able to forgive you," or, "You're ruined for life. God can't do anything with a mess like you"?

Don't ever listen to those lies. God says He forgives your confessed sin and won't even remember it again. He doesn't just put all the smutty contents of your sin in an envelope so you look perfectly good on the outside. He *removes* your sin and actually makes you pure and righteous.

Moses didn't run around, saying, "But I killed a man in Egypt, so there's no way that God can use me." Moses knew how to accept God's forgiveness, to live close to God, and to let God do miraculous things through him.

Peter didn't keep reminding himself that he had denied Jesus at the time when Jesus needed him most. Peter lived like a forgiven man, and that made all the difference. With forgiveness comes God's love, joy, and power to defeat sin. Of course, the earthly consequences of sin will still be around—the murdered man will still be dead, the murderer will still be in jail, the illegitimate child will keep asking questions, and the person you've hurt deeply may not forgive you. But God in His wisdom and mercy can work His miracles in all of this—if you let Him. A former murderer who lives like a forgiven man, displaying real joy and peace, even in jail, may be one of God's best advertisements. Give God a chance with your life.

"For I will be merciful toward their iniquities, and I will remember their sins no more" (Heb. 8:12).

"As far as the east is from the west, so far does he remove our transgressions from us" (Ps. 103:12).

"He will again have compassion upon us, he will tread our iniquities under foot. Thou wilt cast all our sins into the depths of the sea" (Mic. 7:19).

1. List the figures of speech, or examples, used to explain what God does to our sins when He forgives them.
2. How does God feel toward a person who comes to Him for forgiveness?
3. Think back on any sins you're committed in the last week. Con-

fess them to the Lord, and then imagine them being buried in the darkest, deepest ocean bottom (Mic. 7:19).

Perfectly Clean

If I were sending a five-year-old girl out to play in a yard still filled with puddles from last night's rain, I'd give her clear instructions: "Now don't play in the mud and don't get your teddy bear dirty." If she were an ordinary five-year-old, she'd probably come back into the house covered with mud, and crying, "I'm really sorry. I didn't mean to do it. Please don't spank me."

I could reply, "That's okay, dear. I accept you and forgive you just the way you are." But forgiving her wouldn't be enough. She would still be a mess. Because she was already so dirty, she'd have no reason to stop playing in the mud. And there are lots of things that a clean girl can do that a muddy girl cannot do—a clean girl would be allowed to go many places where a dirty girl would not be accepted. Actually, my scrubbing that little girl and giving her clean clothes would make a *change* in her. She would *act* differently once she was clean.

God not only forgives our sin but He also "cleanses us from all unrighteousness." He cleans us up completely. This is not something we can do for ourselves, but we do have a part. The five-year-old cannot do an adequate job of washing herself and providing herself with clean clothes. However, she must co-operate with the person who is bathing her and giving her a fresh change of clothes. Let God cleanse you from the inside out and make you a new and a clean person. The more you long for a clean, pure life, the deeper His cleansing will be.

"If we confess ours sins, he is faithful and just, and will forgive our sins and cleanse us from all unrighteousness" (1 John 1:9).

"How much more shall the blood of Christ, who through the eternal Spirit offered himself without blemish to God, purify your conscience from dead works to serve the living God" (Heb. 9:14).

"In a great house there are not only vessels of gold and silver but also of wood and earthenware, and some for noble use, some for ignoble. If any one purifies himself from what is ignoble, then he will be a vessel for noble use, consecrated and useful to the master of the house, ready for any good work. So shun youthful passions and aim at righteousness, faith, love, and peace, along with those who call upon God from a pure heart" (2 Tim. 2:20-22).

1. What is the thing that purifies our consciences?
2. God cleanses us for a purpose. What is that purpose?
3. It is the blood of Jesus that cleans us up, but we have the responsibility of co-operating with Him. What specific things are we told to do?

How Many Times Is Seventy-Times-Seven?

"I don't think I can ever forgive him." Have you ever said or thought that? If you have, you are on dangerous ground. The verses that come just after the Lord's Prayer in the Sermon on the Mount are not recited by church congregations, or used often as sermon texts, but they are just as much a part of the Bible.

"For if you forgive men their trespasses, your heavenly Father also will forgive you; but if you do not forgive men their trespasses, neither will your father forgive your trespasses" (Matt. 6:14, 15).

If you are a Christian, *you must forgive*. When Jesus, the perfect Son of God, forgave you for everything you've ever done, how can you not forgive another person—no matter what he has done? Your emotions may not be completely under your control, but if, by an act of your will, you choose to forgive, your feelings will sooner or later come into line.

God cannot forgive you if you refuse to forgive others. The Christian with an unforgiving attitude walks straight into trouble—God won't let His children get by with unforgiving attitudes. Peter thought he was being very generous if he forgave a person for the same offense seven times. How many times has God forgiven you?

"Then Peter came up and said to him, 'Lord, how often shall my brother sin against me, and I forgive him? As many as seven times?' Jesus said to him, 'I do not say to you seven times, but seventy times seven.' . . . then his lord summoned him and said to him, 'You wicked servant! I forgave you all that debt because you besought me; and should not you have had mercy on your fellow servant, as I had mercy on you? And in anger his lord delivered him to the jailers, till he should pay all his debt. So also my heavenly Father will do to every one of you, if you do not forgive your brother from your heart" (Matt. 18:21, 22, 32-35).

1. What should you do if someone wrongs you and is unwilling even to apologize?

2. What kind of forgiveness does God expect us to give?
3. How will God deal with us if we refuse to forgive?

Are You Forgiving Yourself?

When I was young, my cousin came one day to play with my sister and me. In her excitement, my sister told him about the bedroom slippers with bunnies on them which he would be receiving for Christmas. Suddenly remembering that this was a secret, she said, "Forget that I ever told you."

The next time we visited my cousin's home, he assured my sister, "I forgot all about the slippers with bunnies on them that you're going to give me for Christmas."

Is your attitude toward God's forgiveness of your confessed sin influenced by similar experiences you've had with people? Do you really believe that God means it when He says that He will forgive *all* your sin? He does mean it. Confess your sin with complete trust that God will destroy it in the fire of His holiness.

Some people say, "Well, I know that God forgives me, but I can't forgive myself." Since when have you been in the business of forgiving your own sins? Only the extreme pride of putting yourself above God could make you think you're responsible for forgiving your own sins. God says He'll not only forgive your sin, but He'll forget it. Not taking God at His word is unbelief. Accept His forgiveness.

"I, I am He who blots out your transgressions for my own sake, and I will not remember your sins" (Isa. 43:25).

"I thank him who has given me strength for this, Christ Jesus our Lord, because he judged me faithful by appointing me to his service, though I formerly blasphemed and persecuted and insulted him; but I received mercy because I had acted ignorantly in unbelief, and the grace of our Lord overflowed for me with the faith and love that are in Christ Jesus. The saying is sure and worthy of full acceptance, that Christ Jesus came into the world to save sinners. And I am the foremost of sinners" (1 Tim. 1:12-15).

1. What kinds of sins had Paul committed?
2. What things had Jesus done for Paul?
3. How can God's willingness to forgive Paul encourage you?

Forgiven Sinners, Inc.

I wish I could have seen Jesus heal a blind man, or raise Lazarus from the dead. Yet, the miracle of Jesus' forgiving and changing the repentant sinner outranks all others. David committed both adultery and murder, but because of his full and sincere confession, he received forgiveness, and God was able to use him to rule His people and write part of the Bible.

As a boy St. Augustine had taken part in a theft, and as a young man he had lived with his girlfriend, an arrangement acceptable to most of Roman society. After he became a Christian, Augustine lived a holy life that others admired, and he became a brilliant writer and church leader. When he was dying, he asked that Psalm 32 be printed in large letters and hung above his bed so he could read the words and meditate on them. The Psalm begins:

"Blessed is he whose transgression is forgiven, whose sin is covered" (Ps. 32:1).

It's easy to forget that Jesus taught that visible sins are a result of wrong thinking, and that we are responsible for our *thoughts* as well as our *actions*. Therefore, we tend to think that only ex-cons have experienced great forgiveness. But if a film were made of your thought life, would it be an X-rated movie? All of us need mountains of God's forgiveness. Forgiven sinners are amazing miracles. If you're not one of the group, join 'em!

"Then turning toward the woman he said to Simon, 'Do you see this woman? I entered your house, you gave me no water for my feet, but she has wet my feet with her tears and wiped them with her hair. You gave me no kiss, but from the time I came in she has not ceased to kiss my feet. You did not anoint my head with oil, but she has anointed my feet with ointment. Therefore I tell you, her sins, which are many, are forgiven, for she loved much; but he who is forgiven little, loves little' " (Luke 7:44-47).

1. If you have been forgiven of little, is it because you haven't sinned much, or because you haven't bothered to confess the sins you have committed?
2. Why will the truly forgiven person love Jesus so much?
3. What are some of the blessings of forgiveness?

No Unfinished Projects

Some of my Christian friends wear buttons that say, "Please be patient, God isn't finished with me yet." It's wonderful to know that God doesn't just forgive us and then leave us alone. Also, He won't suddenly abandon us to work on more promising Christians. The work which God began in you the day you accepted Christ as your Savior, He continues every day of your life and will one day complete in heaven.

God wants to care for everything in your life—temporal or spiritual—because it will affect you for eternity. He will silently continue working in you every moment. All this will happen on one condition—that you trust Him. Absolute trust in God has been the key factor in the lives of people God has mightily used. They weren't the most talented people. Often they didn't possess great charm and wit. They even made mistakes that some other Christians would not have made. But, through it all they trusted God to work in them, and God fulfilled His purposes in their lives.

The devil wants to prevent the work of God in your life, and He has some very sneaky ways of doing it. He tries to convince you that it's humble to say or think, "I'm such a poor Christian, I could never work for God," or, "Other people can pray, or witness, or lead a Bible study so much better, so I'll let them do it," or, "I've had such a bad background so the devil especially picks on me. I don't have much chance to grow as a Christian." These are not humble confessions. They are *insults* to God who can do the impossible. He is waiting for you to trust Him enough to take your hands off and let Him work in your life.

"The Lord will fulfill his purpose for me" (Ps. 138:8).

"For I know the plans I have for you, says the Lord, plans for welfare and not for evil, to give you a future and a hope" (Jer. 29:11).

"And I am sure that he who began a good work in you will bring it to completion at the day of Jesus Christ" (Phil. 1:6).

1. Who will take the responsibility for making sure you develop into a mature Christian?
2. What is your part in all this?
3. Why shouldn't you allow "bad" circumstances to get you down?

God Even Used Peter's Big Mouth

A lot of teenagers could identify with the Apostle Peter. He was a jump-in-before-you-think loud-mouth who couldn't be depended on. He loved to let people know he was around and wanted to be an authority on topics about which he knew very little. Peter was born with some great natural abilities and characteristics, but his wrong motives made them completely useless to Jesus.

People must have wondered what Jesus saw in him, but He loved Peter and forgave him. Peter accepted this forgiveness and gave his life to Jesus. When Jesus put the right motives within Peter, his willingness to jump into anything became courage, his love for talking was transformed into ability to *preach*—and God made him dependable. Everyone else would have laughed if Jesus had predicted the great things Peter would do.

Jesus never gave up on Peter; He saw his potential. Jesus sees what you can be and He won't give up on you—trust Him. If you fail, it's not because you are ugly, or have an offensive personality, or are stupid, or have horrible parents. It's because you didn't let Jesus give you His motives and you didn't expect miracles in your life. In order to receive Jesus' motives, you must confess your sin and yield to His correction. Then accept His forgiveness and wait in faith to see what God can do with your big mouth or your poor study habits.

"Simon, Simon, behold, Satan demanded to have you, that he might sift you like wheat, but I have prayed for you that your faith may not fail; and when you have turned again, strengthen your brethren" (Luke 22:31, 32).

"But Peter, standing with the eleven, lifted up his voice and addressed them, 'Men of Judea and all who dwell in Jerusalem, let this be known to you, and give ear to my words. . . . Let all the house of Israel therefore know assuredly that God has made him both Lord and Christ, this Jesus whom you crucified.' Now when they heard this they were cut to the heart, and said to Peter and the rest of the apostles, 'Brethren, what shall we do?' And Peter said to them, 'Repent, and be baptized every one of you in the name of Jesus Christ for the forgiveness of your sins; and you shall receive the gift of the Holy Spirit' " (Acts 2:14, 36-38).

1. Why did the sermon Peter preached on the day of Pentecost take a lot of courage?
2. Where did Peter receive the ability and the fearlessness he displayed that day?
3. Is there a situation you must soon face that demands more ability and courage than you already have? What should you do about it?

Week Seven

QUIT SINNING AND START WINNING

Do You Send Invitations to Temptation?

A little boy who lived near a lake was instructed by his father to never go swimming without supervision. One day his father caught him swimming. Soon the innocent-sounding little guy was saying, "But, Daddy, I didn't mean to go swimming. It just happened."

"Then," replied his father, "why did you take your swim suit with you when you came to play near the lake?"

The little boy answered, "I took it along just in case I got tempted."

Are you like that little boy? Do you devise plans that will make it harder for you to obey Jesus' commands, even though you say you love Him? Instead of providing yourself with the possibility for sinning, give yourself every opportunity to do right. If the little boy had worn his new watch and left his swim suit at home, the day would have ended differently.

Take Jesus with you through the day and think, "How would He plan for this situation?" Jesus wouldn't even consider lying his way out of an uncomfortable situation. Realizing this, honestly face the problem at hand. You know that Jesus would have you plan a date carefully to avoid situations in which temptation could become strong. Jesus would study for the test instead of trying to pick up some answers at lunch from a friend who took the test second hour.

If you give yourself to Jesus, He'll show you how to organize your life so that obeying God's commandments will be easier.

"But put on the Lord Jesus Christ, and make no provision for the flesh, to gratify [fulfill] its desires" (Rom. 13:14).

"And after a time his master's wife cast her eyes upon Joseph, and said, 'Lie with me.' But he refused and said to his master's wife, '. . . How then can I do this great wickedness, and sin against God?' And although she spoke to Joseph day after day, he would not listen to her, to lie with her or to be with her. But one day, when he went into the house to do his work and none of the men of the house was there in the house, she caught him by his garment, saying, 'Lie with me.' But he left his garment in her hand, and fled and got out of the house" (Gen. 39:7-12).

1. What was Joseph's answer to Mrs. Potiphar the first time she asked him to go to bed with her?
2. What measures did Joseph take to avoid temptation?
3. What ways can you think of to avoid especially difficult temptations?

Choosing Right

If for some strange reason I wanted to rid America of Coca Cola, it would be ridiculous for me to start by defacing every Coca Cola sign I could find. Even smashing Coke bottles and burying Coke cans wouldn't be very effective. I'd have to demolish every factory and destroy every recipe to effectively do the job.

When it comes to fighting sin, man tries to overcome sin by bits and pieces—smashing Coke bottles if you will—without dealing with the source. The blood of Jesus takes away sins, but the cross has also dealt with the sinful self which is the source of sin. In your own strength, you can't die to sin and live to righteousness. You must give yourself completely to God so that His power *within* you can make you strong against temptation. God has promised that He'll never let you face a temptation too strong for you, and He will always provide a way of escape.

Have this attitude: My eyes belong to Jesus and therefore it's impossible for them to look at an X-rated movie; my mouth belongs to Jesus who wouldn't think of spreading this gossip; my hands belong to Jesus so they'll be glad to do the dishes because my mother looks tired tonight. This isn't just the power of positive thinking. Only God can work like this in your life. Memorize one of the scripture verses for today and keep asking God to show you what it means for your life.

"He himself bore our sins in his body on the tree, that we might die to sin and live to righteousness" (1 Pet. 2:24).

"Put off your old nature which belongs to your former manner of life and is corrupt through deceitful lusts, and be renewed in the spirit of your minds, and put on the new nature, created after the likeness of God in true righteousness and holiness" (Eph. 4:22-24).

1. What are we to take off in the same way we take off dirty clothes? Remember that throwing away the old sinful you isn't enough—you must replace it with something better. You must constantly expose your mind to God's truth and let that rule you rather than the world's thinking.
2. After taking off the "dirty clothes" of our sin, what are we to put on?
3. Peter writes that we can "die to sin." What are some characteristics of being dead?

Right and Wrong

When God gives us commands, He gives us the power to obey. He wants us to have victory over sin. A lot of our frustration comes because we are confused about what sin really is, and how we can overcome it. God *doesn't* command us to look sharp at all times, appear successful, never be clumsy, and always please everyone. God does command us to "Honor your father and mother," "Be still and know that I am God," "Trust in the Lord with all your heart," and "If possible so far as it depends on you, live peaceably with all."

Victory involves moment-by-moment decisions to apologize to your mother, to concentrate on God's power rather than on the unfair decision, to determine to trust God for the money you need to attend camp, and to be a good worker for the crabby boss. Maintaining an image of a person who never makes mistakes has nothing to do with victory over sin.

Also understand that there is a big difference between willfully disobeying God and unconsciously sinning. In fact, many people define sin as "willful disobedience to God." Every person who has taken care of little children knows the difference between a child purposely disobeying a specific command such as, "You must not play in the sandbox with your good clothes on," and a child in his excitement forgetting that the cement is wet and cannot be walked on. Our humanness may prevent us from doing all God wishes; but if we set our wills toward obeying Him, He will always give us the power to obey His specific commands. That power to obey comes from God who has all power.

"No temptation has overtaken you that is not common to man. God is faithful, and he will not let you be tempted beyond your strength, but with the temptation will also provide the way of escape that you may be able to endure it" (1 Cor. 10:13).

"But now put them all away; anger, wrath, malice, slander, and foul talk from your mouth. Do not lie to one another, seeing that you have put off the old nature with its practices and have put on the new nature, which is being renewed in knowledge after the image of its creator. Put on then, as God's chosen ones, holy and beloved, compassion, kindness, lowliness, meekness, and patience, forbearing one another and, if one has a complaint against another, forgiving each other; as the Lord has forgiven you, so you also must forgive. And above all these put on love, which binds everything together in perfect harmony" (Col. 3:8-10, 12-14).

1. What are we told to do with sinful practices and thoughts?
2. List the things that Christians are specifically told to put on and wear. Are these part of your "wardrobe"?

That Selfishness Inside Me

The basic problem is, "How do I get rid of the selfish me that wants its own way and gets into arguments with God?" *God has provided a way*. Paul writes: "But far be it from me to glory except in the cross of our Lord Jesus Christ, by which the world has been crucified to me, and I to the world" (Gal. 6:14).

Crucifixion means death. Since we have proven ourselves to be sinners, there is no way for that sinful self to be eradicated unless it dies. The miracle of the cross is that not only did Jesus shed His blood to take away our sins but that sinful self within us was crucified when Jesus died. When Paul says, "I have been crucified with Christ," he means exactly that.

Just as Jesus' blood doesn't cleanse your sin unless you have faith in that fact and ask for forgiveness, so too, the death of your old sinful self becomes real in you only if you allow it. A cruel slave master wouldn't be able to make a dead slave do anything—no matter how viciously he tortured him. Sin, like that cruel master, is always trying to enslave you. But by giving up your right to have your own way, and surrendering totally to Jesus, you can by faith make the miracle of the cross—"by which the world has been crucified to me and I to the world"—real in your life.

If I give up my right to have everyone think my piano solo was the highlight of the evening, and have faith that God can work in my life through every situation, I don't have to be angry because my number is omitted from the program. The selfish me is dead, and circumstances don't have to cause me to sin.

Know that Jesus took your old self with Him to the cross. Give your will to God. Believe that God can do in you what you can't do yourself.

"Truly, truly, I say to you, unless a grain of wheat falls into the earth and dies, it remains alone; but if it dies, it bears much fruit. He who loves his life loses it, and he who hates his life in this world will keep it for eternal life. If any one serves me, he must follow me; and where I am, there shall my servant be also; if anyone serves me, the Father will honor him" (John 12:24-26).

1. What excuses could a grain of wheat have for not being buried in the ground?
2. What excuses do you have for not giving yourself totally to God?

Caterpillars Can Change

Do you ever feel like you're caught in quicksand, a slimey bog, a bottomless pit—a situation you don't think you'll ever be able to get out of? Well, the Bible calls this kind of vicious circle the law of sin and death. There are basically two laws—the law of the Spirit of life in Christ, and the law of sin and death. There is our selfish nature with its inability to obey and love God, and there is God's nature which loves freely and sets us free from the power of our old nature.

How can one get free from the law of sin and death? Caterpillars have a pretty rough time getting through mud without getting soiled by it. Let's say that the mud is sin. Mud is everywhere and it seems impossible to avoid. The caterpillar can't rise above the mud either—unless it can get rid of its caterpillar self. This, of course, can happen if the caterpillar's old self is discarded and the creature becomes a beautiful butterfly.

Now if the caterpillar had a choice in this matter and could say, "I want to remain a caterpillar because I like the mud and it's just caterpillar nature to like mud," there would be no victory and no flying above mud. You are faced with the same choice: you can choose to live by God's law and become a butterfly, or you can live by the law of sin and death and crawl like a caterpillar.

"For the law of the Spirit of life in Christ Jesus has set me free from the law of sin and death" (Rom. 8:2).

"For those who live according to the flesh set their minds on the things of the flesh, but those who live according to the Spirit set their minds on the things of the Spirit. To set the mind on the flesh is death, but to set the mind on the Spirit is life and peace. For the mind that is set on the flesh is hostile to God; it does not submit to God's law, indeed it cannot; and those who are in the flesh cannot please God. But you are not in the flesh, you are in the Spirit, if in fact the Spirit of God dwells in you. Any one who does not have the Spirit of Christ does not belong to him" (Rom. 8:5-9).

1. What does it mean to "set the mind" on something?
2. How can you set your mind on the Spirit?
3. What problem in your life will require setting your mind on the Spirit if the problem is going to be solved?

Faith and Sin Can't Sit on the Same Bench

One definition of faith goes like this: "Faith is my acceptance of God's fact." The devil is always trying to get you to doubt truth. But your disbelief of a fact doesn't make it false, it simply becomes inoperative in your life. It is just as possible to walk across a plank which connects the roofs of two five-story buildings as it is to cross one laid on the ground. However, lack of belief in that fact, and fear based on lack of faith, will keep one from doing so.

One important Bible fact is, "No one born of God commits sin; for God's nature abides in him, and he cannot sin because he is born of God" (1 John 3:9). Watchman Nee explains, "John is not telling us that sin is now no longer in our history and that we shall not again commit sin. He is saying that to sin is not in the nature of that which is born of God." In nature wood floats, but in history it is possible for wood to sink if it is enclosed in metal or if it is nailed to a dock which is under water.

Now I have a choice. Will I live by God's fact—"Whatsoever is born of God cannot sin," or by what my experience seems to show? If I were blind, I couldn't see a sunset, and if I were deaf, I couldn't enjoy a concert. Yet, the elegance of the colors and the beauty of the music would still exist even if I couldn't make them part of my experience. The piece of wood encased in metal may stay in the bottom of a lake until it rots not knowing it's nature is to float. Even so, the devil may deceive you into thinking there is no deliverance from the power of sin. If you don't believe "no one born of God commits sin," you live as though that page of your Bible didn't exist.

Fact, Faith, and Experience were walking along the top of a wall. As long as Faith followed Fact, everything was fine. But when Faith looked back to see how Experience was doing, he nearly fell off. Put your faith in God's facts, not in your experience or feelings.

"By this we know that we love the children of God, when we love God and obey his commandments. For this is the love of God, that we keep his commandments. And his commandments are not burdensome. For whatever is born of God overcomes the world; and this is the victory that overcomes the world, our faith. Who is it that overcomes the world but he who believes that Jesus is the Son of God?" (1 John 5:2-5).

1. What is automatically expected of people who love God?
2. What is necessary if we are to overcome the world and have victory?

3. Why is belief that Jesus is the Son of God crucial to victory in your life?

But You Could Fly

The Bible talks about two kinds of life—the life of the spirit and the life of the flesh—natural life. We're living in a world where the things around us are running according to natural life—the life of the flesh. It's a world in which people are expected to stomp on others to get to the top, to tell lies when a lot is at stake, and to boast about how great they are.

When you become a Christian and start reading the Bible, you learn about selflessness, truth, and humility. The person who uses the resources available in natural life to try to turn the other cheek and love his enemies will give up in frustration. But God has given His children Spirit life, and Spirit life can do what natural life—the life of the flesh—can never accomplish. For example, the law of gravity governs our earth. Whether I throw an algebra book out the window on the eighty-seventh floor (Wouldn't you like to sometimes?) or merely drop a pencil, gravity will take over. However, there are other physical laws. Looking up in the sky, you'll have to admit that neither birds nor airplanes seem to worry about the law of gravity. They fly according to a higher law.

If science fiction writers concocted a power which enabled individuals to fly three hundred miles per hour and land safely, just by carrying a pocket-size device, readers would be amazed if this power were never used. Obviously, the person who has never accepted Christ in the first place doesn't have the life of the Spirit to give power. However, there are Christians who never use the supernatural Spirit-power they possess. If we try to follow God's rules in our own strength, we are doomed to failure. The devil knows this and is always trying to make us depend on our own strength. If you rely on the supernatural life of Jesus' Spirit, you'll be flying above temptations to sin, but if you trust yourself, you're bound to crash.

"Not by might, nor by power, but by my Spirit, says the Lord of hosts" (Zech. 4:6).

"But if Christ is in you, although your bodies are dead because of sin, your spirits are alive because of righteousness. If the Spirit of him who raised Jesus from the dead dwells in you, he who raised Christ Jesus from the dead will give life to your mortal bodies also through his Spirit which dwells in you. So then, brethren, we are debtors, not to the flesh, to live according to the flesh—for if you live according to the flesh, you will die, but if by the Spirit you put to death the deeds of the body you will live. For all who are led by the Spirit of God are sons of God" (Rom. 8:10-14).

1. What great thing did the Holy Spirit do in history (Rom. 8:11)?
2. What is the difference between meeting temptation in our own power and in the power of the Holy Spirit?
3. What problem in your life have you been trying to solve with your own power?

Week Eight

ME, MYSELF, AND I—YOUR
SELF-IMAGE

Who Am I Anyway?

You came to God as a dirty, rotten sinner whose righteousness is no better than filthy rags, unable to save yourself. Then how do you square that with the fact that God created you to be something special and that you should accept yourself? You really can thank God that you have knobby knees, red hair and freckles, and at the same time confess to Him that your motives are selfish and need to be changed by Him—if you're willing to accept God's definition of who you are.

My car is a good little car—it runs well, doesn't have any big dents, and requires very little repair. However, one Sunday morning there was an incredibly heavy rainfall which turned every low area in the city into a lake. When my car came to the waist-deep water under a railroad bridge, it was totally helpless, as were all the other cars. One driver thought his car should be able to double as a boat and went full speed into that deep water. Of course, his car stopped and nearly drowned!

What if that poor car, nearly covered by water, began thinking, *I'm a total failure because here I am in all this water and I can't do a thing. I'm awful*? We'd think it was pretty dumb for a car to be depressed because it couldn't function as a boat. Now the Bible teaches that Jesus has to enter our lives and change us from the inside out. When you get discouraged because you are not naturally good, you are like the car trying to be a boat. Just as the car could be thankful that it was a compact that saved on gas, that it was painted red, and that it had a vinyl interior, so you should be thankful for the way God made you—for the unique qualities you have and for the special ways you can be of service to God.

You are important to God and He loves you very much. That's why He sent Jesus to save you. But your natural "goodness" does not impress God, and you can't save yourself. Even after you become a Christian, you can't live the Christian life in your own strength.

"We have all become like one who is unclean, and all our righteous deeds are like a polluted garment" (Isa. 64:6).

"I have loved you with an everlasting love; therefore I have continued my faithfulness to you" (Jer. 31:3).

"For I know that nothing good dwells within me" (Rom. 7:18).

"But by the grace of God I am what I am" (1 Cor. 15:10).

1. As God looks at you, what characteristics—good and bad—does He see?
2. If you were God, able to see into every corner of everyone's life, would you love you?
3. Describe the kind of love God has for you.

God Loves You—Pimples and All

If you possessed the power to change anything about the way you look, would you use that power? Would you like to have a shorter nose, thinner legs, fewer freckles, or smaller feet? Most people would answer "yes" to this question, but in answering "yes" they are forgetting some important things. Why does almost every person wish to be cast in the beauty queen or the Mr. America mold? It's only because right now that is the world's definition of "beautiful" or "handsome." However, popular standards of beauty change; a woman with a tan was once considered ugly, and the somewhat hefty Statue of Liberty was once considered the ideal feminine form!

God wants you to accept His definition of "beautiful," and He wants to make you beautiful from the *inside* out. God made you just the way you are so you could best reflect His beauty. A problem with wanting to remake yourself is that you're actually telling God that He did a bad job when He created you. You don't like it when people tell you *your* painting or cake is the worst they've ever seen; the Master Designer of the Universe doesn't exactly appreciate nasty comments from you either.

You'll enjoy a great sense of relaxation and peace when you accept yourself the way God made you. After you have done this, ask God what things you can do to look your best. A diet, more exercise, or a change of hair style may be in God's plan for you. Accepting the way God made you, and thanking Him for it, will save you from one of two extremes: not caring about your appearance because you think you're so ugly it won't help, or spending too much time and money trying to look acceptable.

"For thou didst form my inward parts, thou didst knit me together in my mother's womb. I praise thee, for thou art fearful and wonderful. Wonderful are thy works. Thou knowest me right well; my frame was not hidden from thee, when I was being made in secret, intricately wrought in the depths of the earth. Thy eyes beheld my unformed substance; in thy book were written every one of them, the days that were formed for me, when as yet there were none of them" (Ps. 139:13-16).

"He has made everything beautiful" (Eccles. 3:11).

1. Each of us can say the things that David said in Psalm 139. What things did God plan for you before you were born?
2. Why did the Psalmist thank God for the way he was made?
3. Have you thanked God for making you just the way you are?

Self-image

Do you ever feel worthless? Do zits, greasy hair, and a lack of poise get you down? Do you dwell on the fact that you are unco-ordinated or a poor student, or are not particularly popular? You need this very old truth from the Bible: "For the Lord sees not as man sees; man looks on the outward appearance, but the Lord looks on the heart" (1 Sam. 16:7).

Getting out of the low self-image syndrome involves deciding who is important to you and who is going to shape your image of yourself. If you let society do it, you will always come out a loser because no one can be good-looking, witty, successful, intelligent, athletic, musical, and well informed, all at the same time. Every other TV commercial warns that you are lacking in some way. You could let your friends shape your self-image, but conforming to the crowd has its dangers. Besides, your friends could let you down.

You may think you would feel good about yourself if you fell in love and a special person would believe in you. However, married people usually seem just as insecure as those who are single, and lovers often turn into people who compete with each other and tear each other down. Some of you don't even look for acceptance in your family, though others can see that your family seems to love you most when you're simply doing what is expected of you.

If you decide that God is going to be so important in your life that nothing else matters, you'll sense God loving you and comforting you when no one else understands. The God who made the universe, controls the galaxies, and presides over history loves you—warts and all—with a constant love. In the light of this great fact, should what other people think of you be that important? If God is really first in your life, the opinions of others will never ruin your self-image.

"Nevertheless I am continually with thee; thou dost hold my right hand. Thou dost guide me with thy counsel, and afterward thou wilt receive me to glory. Whom have I in heaven but thee? And there is nothing upon earth that I desire besides thee. My flesh and my heart may fail, but God is the strength of my heart and my portion forever" (Ps. 73:23-26).

1. On a scale of one to ten, how would the writer of this Psalm rate God?
2. How can God's nearness and His importance make the difference

next time you make a fool of yourself in front of the most popular kids in school?

3. Do you spend more time being concerned about the inside of you that God sees, or the outside which others see?

Self-consciousness

One definition of self-consciousness is "thinking about yourself." How much time do you waste worrying about how you look, wondering if others have a good impression of you, or trying to analyze why your feelings are hurt. Self-consciousness can keep a talented pianist from ever performing in front of a group, prevent a guy from giving a word of encouragement or affection, or stop someone from learning to ski. Every time we start thinking only about ourselves we spend time in self-pity, which can only hurt us.

You may agree that self-consciousness is bad and that you'd love to forget about how you look to others; you really want to ignore ridicule, and you would like to try new things that you may not be able to do well. The question you have is, "How can I live above self-consciousness?"

There's a man in the Bible who had self-consciousness licked. Sure, some people made fun of him. After all, camel's hair T-shirts weren't high fashion, and the Roman emperor didn't eat locusts and wild honey for breakfast. Living in the desert wasn't the thing to do either. But John the Baptist had something, and his preaching was worth listening to—even worth going out to the desert to hear. The fact that he was losing all his disciples to Jesus didn't bother him either. He had learned to replace self-consciousness with Christ-consciousness.

It is impossible to really concentrate on two things at once. If you are only aware of serving Christ and living for Him, self-consciousness will disappear. John the Baptist thought so much of Jesus that he described Him as One "the thong of whose sandal I am not worthy to untie."

When self-consciousness comes to haunt you, always ask the question, "Whom am I living for anyway—God or myself?"

"Then I said, 'Ah, Lord God! Behold, I do not know how to speak, for I am only a youth.' But the Lord said to me, 'Do not say, "I am only a youth"; for to all to whom I send you you shall go, and whatever I command you you shall speak. Be not afraid of them, for I am with you to deliver you. . . . But you, gird up your loins; arise, and say to them everything that I command you. Do not be dis-

mayed by them, lest I dismay you before them' " (Jer. 1:6-8, 17).
"He must increase but I must decrease" (John 3:30).

1. What does God say about Jeremiah's self-conscious attitude?
2. In light of God's advice to Jeremiah in verse 17, what would you tell a Christian friend of yours who is scared to death to give a report in tomorrow's English class?

Lions, Losers, and Lessons

Paul's situation in Rome was "the pits"—and then some. He was in prison and his only "crime" was preaching the good news of Jesus Christ. Almost all of his friends had deserted him, and at his trial no one defended him. Even though he had not been fed to the lions this time, a shortage of criminals to execute at the next Colosseum show could affect the outcome of a future court hearing. He didn't even have his coat and his books.

Most people in a situation like this would have written, "Everything I've ever lived for is gone. I'm a miserable failure and there is no one to cheer me up." Instead, Paul wrote that he had fought a good fight, he had kept the faith, and he was praising the Lord. Paul knew that success was obeying God, regardless of how things turn out.

A lot of frustration comes from your deciding you're a failure because you didn't measure up to your own goals or the expectations someone else made for you. How about learning a lesson from Paul? How about measuring success and failure by God's standards? If you are disobeying God, you may look very successful but you are still a failure. If you are wholeheartedly obeying God, you are a success—even if all your report card grades are below C level.

"For I am already on the point of being sacrificed; the time of my departure has come. I have fought the good fight, I have finished the race, I have kept the faith. Henceforth, there is laid up for me the crown of righteousness, which the Lord, the righteous judge, will award to me on that Day, and not only to me but also to all who have loved his appearing" (2 Tim. 4:6-8).

"The Lord will rescue me from every evil and save me for his heavenly kingdom. To him be the glory for ever and ever" (2 Tim. 4:18).

1. Why was Paul not discouraged?

2. List statements which prove that Paul was not worried about being a failure or being executed.
3. Paul viewed the Christian life as a "fight" and a "race." How do you view the Christian life?

The Right Frame for the Picture

Once you decide to let Jesus be the Lord of your life, you can develop a strategy for coping with feelings of inadequacy and inferiority. The most important consideration is what Jesus thinks and what He wants. That makes you like a picture frame; the beautiful and valuable painting is Jesus within you.

People don't go to art galleries to admire frames. However, it is important that the frame blends with the picture to complement its beauty. God had a plan for you before you were born. Your looks and your personality were especially designed to complement the life of Jesus within you. To the person who puts Jesus first, there is no higher purpose than displaying Jesus. If someone says of you, "If a person like that can be a Christian, I can too," your whole life will be worthwhile.

But how does this relate to feeling like an idiot because you struck out again, or feeling self-conscious because everyone else dressed up and you didn't? If Jesus is first in your life, these other things will not be important enough to ruin your day. Constantly carry on a little conversation with Jesus, saying things like, "Well, Lord, if you think I look great, that's good enough for me"; or, "Lord, now that everyone is mad at me for causing the team to lose, I know more about the rejection you faced on earth"; or, "Lord, help me find a person who is hurting on the inside, so I can help that person rather than thinking about my wearing the wrong thing."

Of course, there's nothing especially spiritual about being a bad baseball player or dressing out of place; but how we look or perform is not terribly important. God's "picture frames" should certainly pray about their appearance and the impression they make, but should always remember: "Therefore I tell you, do not be anxious about your life, what you shall eat or what you shall drink, nor about your body, what you shall put on" (Matt. 6:25).

"All thy works shall give thanks to thee, O Lord, and all thy saints shall bless thee! They shall speak of the glory of thy kingdom and tell of thy power, to make known to the sons of men thy mighty deeds, and the glorious splendor of thy kingdom" (Ps. 145:10-12).

"And whatever you do, in word or deed, do everything in the

name of the Lord Jesus, giving thanks to God and the Father through him" (Col. 3:17).

1. In the above verses, what is God commanding you to do?
2. How does doing everything for God's glory help to defeat feelings of inferiority?
3. If you play baseball to bring honor to Jesus, He will understand perfectly if you strike out—it's not a big deal. If you dress to please Jesus, the pressure to look better than everyone else will be gone and you can relax and be yourself. Are you strained and frustrated in some area of your life because you're too concerned about pleasing people?

You Make a Perfect You

Marching with the high school band in a big parade can be exciting and enjoyable—unless you're in the front row marching out of step and you're wearing the last available hat, which would have fit Humpty Dumpty, but which won't stay on your head even though it's stuffed with two newspapers. Well, it happened to me when I had moved to a new high school. After one practice, I was stuck in a parade. The tuba player kept retrieving my hat and I marched out of step for a mile-and-a-half. I cried all the way home because I thought I had ruined the whole parade. I never even suspected the glaring pride involved in my self-evaluation.

We don't recognize that it's pride which makes us so afraid of making fools out of ourselves. It's pride that wants everyone to think I'm graceful, smooth, and cool, and that's why I nearly die when I mess up on making an introduction. It's because of pride that you want everyone to recognize your great intelligence, and that's why you're crushed when you say something dumb and everyone laughs. It's pride that keeps you in front of the mirror for an hour a day, and makes your world cave in when you get a bad haircut.

Pride can easily become your jailer. Pride rattles his chains when you have to give an oral report in science, when you feel only the most expensive clothes would make you look acceptable, or when you don't want anyone to see you play tennis. Pride demands that you be Superman or Wonder Woman. Confess your pride as sin and come into the freedom Jesus wants to give you. The truth is, you make a perfect you.

"Pride goes before destruction, and a haughty spirit before a fall" (Prov. 16:18).

"The pride of your heart has deceived you, you who live in the clefts of the rock, whose dwelling is high, who say in your heart, who will bring me down to the ground? Though you soar aloft like the eagle, though your nest is set among the stars, thence I will bring you down, says the Lord" (Obad. 1:3, 4).

"For by the grace given to me I bid every one among you not to think of himself more highly than he ought to think, but to think with sober judgment, each according to the measure of faith which God has assigned him" (Rom. 12:3).

1. How does pride deceive us?
2. What strains and pressures come to those who decide they must get to the top and stay there?
3. What does God say about pride?
4. How does pride hurt our relationship with God, our dealings with other people, and our self-image?

Week Nine

TAKE A HARD LOOK AT YOURSELF

Who Tells You What to Do?

Someone once said, "Do what you like and pretty soon you won't like what you do." The "let it all hang out" philosophy is likely to get you into a lot of trouble. Saying exactly what you think will not endear you to your sister, and may incur the anger of your mother and your teachers, not to mention your principal. Doing whatever you wish, whenever you wish to do it, may get you acquainted with policemen, probation officers and judges.

Since the "real you" seems to be such a monster, you've probably allowed others to dictate your behavior. You congratulate the homecoming queen and say you're glad she won—even if you think she's the worst possible choice. You feel obligated to pretend you like eating pizza and drinking Coke. When people ask how you are, you answer, "Fine," even if you're on the verge of tears. The hypocrisy of it all is frightening, and the thought of being a "carbon copy teen" doesn't give you any sense of individuality or importance.

What's the way out? Only your Creator knows who the "real you" is. If you give your life to Jesus and determine to obey Him, He'll bring out your true personality. If you ask Him to show you the reason you were put on this earth, and the unique things He wants you to say and do, He'll show you.

If you buy a new gadget, you don't ask it how it's operated. The trial-and-error methods you might devise would most likely break it. The manufacturer's instructions are reliable because *the maker of the machine knows just how it will work best*. God put great thought and love into designing you. How about following His instructions?

"Woe to him who strives with his Maker, an earthen vessel with the potter! Does the clay say to him who fashions it, 'What are you making?' or 'Your work has no handles'? Thus says the Lord, the Holy One of Israel, and his Maker: 'Will you question me about my children, or command me concerning the work of my hands? I made the earth and created man upon it; it was my hands that stretched out the heavens, and I commanded all their host. I have aroused him in righteousness, and I will make straight all his ways; he shall build my city and set my exiles free, not for price or reward,' says the Lord of hosts" (Isa. 45:9, 11-13).

"And now the Lord says, who formed me from the womb to be his servant, to bring Jacob [the nation of Israel] back to him, and that Israel might be gathered to him, for I am honored in the eyes of the Lord, and my God has become my strength" (Isa. 49:5).

1. List appropriate and inappropriate attitudes we can have toward God and explain why each attitude is right or wrong.
2. What job did God have for Isaiah? (See Isa. 49:5.)
3. What kinds of attitudes did God have toward Isaiah?

Are You Starring on Broadway or Being Yourself?

Are you being yourself, or are you constantly trying to impress people? For many people, life is more like acting than living. Putting on a good front is something taught to us by our society. When some girl talks about all the exciting places her new boyfriend has taken her, and asks her friend where her dates have been taking her lately, an honest, "I haven't been on a date for a year" would be unthinkable. It's not easy to admit that you've never even heard of the book that everybody is reading. Not exaggerating about your weekend is equally difficult. Saying, "I studied for the chemistry test and I failed it" takes a lot of guts.

Besides trying to make people think we've done great things, we try to impress people by what we wear and what we own. Probably most people don't enjoy all the time they spend putting on makeup, getting a suntan, or shopping for clothes, but feel they have to maintain a good image. Worse than this, Christians often want to appear more "spiritual" than they actually are. A guy once remarked, "I don't want to take my new Bible to church. The people will think I never read it." Others try to use the right phrases and to go to all the right meetings.

God sees and judges you exactly for what you are. He isn't impressed with a holiness act. Any pretense you make in any area of life blocks communication with God. Besides, acting is hard work. Jesus wants us to be completely honest and to be ourselves. As soon as you stop pretending to be what you are not, the strain goes away.

"Beware of practicing your piety [religious duties or practices] before men in order to be seen by them; for then you will have no reward from your Father who is in heaven" (Matt. 6:1).

"Thus, when you give alms [money to the poor], sound no trumpet before you, as the hyprocrites do in the synagogues and in the streets, that they may be praised by men. Truly, I say to you, they have received their reward. But when you give alms, do not let your left hand know what your right hand is doing, so that your alms may be in secret; and your Father who sees in secret will reward you. But when you pray, go into your room and shut the door and pray to your Father who is in secret; and your Father who sees in secret will reward you. And in praying do not heap up empty phrases as the Gentiles do; for they think that they will be heard for their many words" (Matt. 6:2-4, 6, 7).

1. What problem do we encounter when we want others to see our good deeds?
2. Can you think of any way in which you've been trying to be your own "press agent"? Talk it over with God.
3. How can praying, or witnessing, or giving a testimony be a stage show?

About That Log in Your Eye

If you don't determine to thank God for the way you look, the abilities you have, and the things that happen to you, you're certain to get a "log" in your eye that will keep you from seeing anything clearly. That "log" is jealousy. Jealousy always comes from lack of trust in God—you don't trust that God has a reason for you not dating right now, so you're jealous of the person with a girlfriend or a boyfriend; you don't thank God for your hair, so you're jealous of some beautiful blond; you don't appreciate the clothes you have, so you're jealous of the doctor's daughter's wardrobe; you aren't thankful for the talents God has given you, so you're jealous of the best player on the team.

Every time jealousy raises its ugly head, confess it as sin and determine to be satisfied with what God has given you, and to thank Him for it. Why don't you start with these two practical suggestions? If you find you are jealous of someone right now, decide to pray for that person every day for the next month. This will give you a chance to experience one of God's miracles—a complete attitude change. Second, make a list of all the things you've never thanked God for; then tell God how much you appreciate Him and the things He has given you. Thanklessness is a sin which opens the door to jealousy.

"As they were coming home, when David returned from slaying the Philistine, the women came out of all the cities of Israel, singing and dancing, to meet King Saul, with timbrels, with songs of joy, and with instruments of music. And the women sang to one another as they made merry, 'Saul has slain his thousands, and David his ten thousands.' And Saul was very angry, and this saying displeased him; he said, 'They have ascribed to David ten thousands, and to me they have ascribed thousands; and what more can he have but the kingdom?' And Saul eyed David from that day on" (1 Sam. 18:6-9).

"For where jealousy and selfish ambition exist, there will be disorder and every vile practice" (James 3:16).

1. How should Saul have handled the situation?
2. What did jealousy do to Saul? (Read 1 Samuel 18-31.)
3. Why is jealousy so dangerous?
4. If you thank God for the way He made you and trust Him for what happens to you, why does that cure jealousy?

You're Not Okay, and Neither Am I

The school auditorium is packed with students, parents, relatives, and people from the neighborhood. The graduates march in. Except for the fact that you lost your mortarboard on the way in, and your gown is shocking pink while everyone else's is navy blue, it is an exciting evening and a great way to end your illustrious high school career. Then the principal says in a booming voice, "We are pleased to present 'The Personality Minus Award' for this year's graduating class." He calls out your name and the band plays off-key. You wake up from your nightmare, wondering if that's what everyone thinks of you.

Although you should accept yourself as God made you, there are times that you should not feel good about yourself. You're *not* okay if you are not dependable—you can change that. Saying, "Well, I won't worry about my laziness because that's just the way I am," is just like stating, "I can ignore God's Word, and I don't believe God has the power to change me." You don't just accept the fact that you are always late—you *decide* to start being on time.

God has a lot to say about character development, especially in the book of Proverbs. Every teenager should read Proverbs several times, and follow the advice offered, allowing the Holy Spirit to show specific steps necessary to reach the goal. In tenth grade I read a book called *How to Improve Your Personality*. I remember

thinking, "This book doesn't say one thing that a person who reads the Bible doesn't already know." Don't use accepting yourself as an excuse for the attitudes and actions that God would give you the power to change.

"And we all, with unveiled face, beholding the glory of the Lord, are being changed into his likeness from one degree of glory to another; for this comes from the Lord who is the Spirit" (2 Cor. 3:18).

1. If we put a veil of unbelief, self-centeredness, stubbornness, or something else over our eyes, we'll be prevented from really see-

ing the glory of God and being changed by it. Do you read the
Bible or come to Jesus in prayer wearing any such veil?
2. Do the changes come instantly or in degrees?
3. How will we be changed into the likeness of Christ?
4. Where is the power that changes us?

Whom Do You Look Like?

You may be a rugged individualist, determined to be your own
person and not be like anyone else. However, it can't really be done.
It's a fact that most people are very much like their parents, and often they most resemble the parent they're determined not to copy.
A husband and wife often think very much alike. A teenager reflects
the values of the friends he or she has.

In the final analysis there are only two molds: you can either be
like Jesus or like the world. Jesus and the world are opposites, so it's
an either-or proposition. Being like the world is easy. You absorb
the latest trends of the media, such as the "new" morality, freedom
to do your own "thing," and "pleasure-at-any-price." Behind these
is the overriding emphasis of the world—you are the center of the
universe and everything should revolve around you.

The basic premise of the world, that mankind is the focal point
of everything, always has and always will remain the same. However, the expressions of it will change so fast that in twenty years
you'll be the "older" generation. You will have some choice as to
what part of the world to follow, and which people will mold your
thinking, but you will not be "yourself."

The alternative is to be conformed to the image of Jesus—to not
only pattern yourself after Him but also to allow the living Holy
Spirit to produce the attitudes and actions of Jesus in you. When
that happens, you may not be the most popular person in school—
but so what? Being God's friend has eternal rewards!

"Do not be conformed to this world but be transformed by the
renewal of your mind, that you may prove what is the will of God,
what is good and acceptable and perfect" (Rom. 12:2).

"Now we have received not the spirit of the world, but the Spirit
which is from God, that we might understand the gifts bestowed on
us by God" (1 Cor. 2:12).

"Unfaithful creatures! Do you not know that friendship with the
world is enmity with God? Therefore whoever wishes to be a friend
of the world makes himself an enemy of God" (James 4:4).

1. What is the world like and what should be the Christian's attitude toward it?
2. What are the consequences of being "an enemy of God"?

Walking in the Footsteps of Jesus

Do you resemble Jesus? Maybe answering that question with a "yes" seems impossible to you. Well, the Bible says that God planned long ago that each of us should be like Jesus. God isn't like the people who make all kinds of plans and dreams that they can't possibly fulfill. God has the means and the power to work out his plans.

The Holy Spirit has put within you the characteristics of Jesus, just as a child has within him the characteristics of his parents. However, if a two-week-old baby could leave his or her parents forever, it is extremely doubtful that much more than the physical resemblances would show up. Most little children spend hours imitating their parents, and are extremely successful. They spend so much time with their parents that they are bound to pick up character traits.

The traits of Jesus placed within you by the Holy Spirit at your conversion will never show through unless you strive to be like Jesus. This means willingness to deny the thinking of the world in order to follow the teachings of Jesus. It means spending time—a lot of time—with Jesus. The more time you spend with Him, the more you will think, act, and talk like Him—the perfect Man.

"A disciple is not above his teacher, but every one when he is fully taught will be like his teacher" (Luke 6:40).

"For those whom he foreknew he also predestined to be conformed to the image of his Son, in order that he might be the first-born among many brethren" (Rom. 8:29).

"Be imitators of me, as I am of Christ" (1 Cor. 11:1).

"For to this you have been called, because Christ also suffered for you, leaving you an example, that you should follow in his steps" (1 Pet. 2:21).

"He who says he abides in him ought to walk in the same way in which he walked" (1 John 2:6).

1. Would God keep demanding of us something He would not give us the power to do?

2. Where do we get the power to live as Jesus lived?
3. Is being like Jesus the most important aim in your life, or does that take second place to other goals?
4. List the analogies that explain to us that we are to be like Jesus.

The Treasure Inside You

With only a dime in your pocket, you can be as careless and haphazard as you wish. However, if you were carrying a million dollars in cash to deposit in the bank, your whole attitude would be different. It would be one of great care and soberness because of the importance of your mission.

Do you fully realize who lives in you? In Solomon's time God's presence was in a beautiful temple made of stone, but today, God has made our hearts the place where He lives! If you have been born again of the Spirit of God, you carry God in your heart! This should instill in you a sense of awe and respect. *You are the temple of God.* When it dawns on you that you are indeed the house God lives in, you can do nothing but surrender yourself totally to Him.

Since your heart is Christ's home, He should have control over every part of His house. You no longer have the right to think anything you want to; Jesus has a right to dominate your thoughts. What God's temple looks like on the outside is no longer determined by your taste and your sense of style; what you wear must be acceptable to Jesus. God's temple can't be as lazy as it wants to be; God gets to reform the work habits of His temple.

In addition to moving you to submit totally to God, realizing that you are God's temple will give you a sense of value because you have a great God inside you. You don't have to feel worthless and ugly. Having God live within you is the greatest privilege in the world.

"Do you not know that your body is a temple of the Holy Spirit within you, which you have from God? You are not your own; you were bought with a price. So glorify God in your body" (1 Cor. 6:19, 20).

"So then you are no longer strangers and sojourners, but you are fellow citizens with the saints and members of the household of God, built upon the foundation of the apostles and prophets, Christ Jesus himself being the cornerstone, in whom the whole structure is joined together and grows into a holy temple in the Lord; in whom you also are built into it for a dwelling place of God in the Spirit" (Eph. 2:19-22).

1. What are the right reasons for you to have a feeling of importance and "belonging"? What are some wrong reasons?
2. Your body is a "little temple" of God, but it joins with all other Christians to make the "big temple" of God. Who must direct the way this living temple fits together and grows?
3. What responsibilities do you have to both the "big temple" and the "little temple" of God?
4. Which is more important, the inside or the outside of the temple?

Week Ten

GOD *DOES* LOVE YOU!

Nobody Loves Me

Have you ever wondered if God *really* loves you? Or maybe you've talked to someone who has serious doubts about God's love for him. A friend of mine received a call from a nurse at a local hospital. She was afraid that an eighteen-year-old patient of hers might die because he had absolutely no desire to live.

A talk with the boy revealed that he had suffered a crippling disease as a child but had, by constant exercise and work, not only learned to walk again, but to run, and excel in athletics. He was now in the hospital as a result of a terrible automobile accident which had killed everyone else in his family. He had suffered severe injuries, but the doctors told him if he worked hard he had a chance of walking again. This young man would not believe that God loved him.

My friend took his Bible and read to him the story of the trial and crucifixion of Jesus. After he finished he asked gently, "Don't you think the God who sent Jesus to suffer and die for you really does love you?" The boy agreed.

You may not understand anything that has happened to you, what you are going through now, or what the future will hold, but the crown of thorns, the spear in His side, and the nails in His hands forever say, "I love you."

"Then the soldiers of the governor took Jesus into the praetorium, and they gathered the whole battalion before him. And they stripped him and put a scarlet robe upon him, and plaiting a crown of thorns they put it on his head, and put a reed in his right hand. And kneeling before him they mocked him, saying, 'Hail, King of the Jews!' And they spat upon him, and took the reed and struck him on the head. And when they had mocked him, they stripped him of the robe, and put his own clothes on him, and led him away to crucify him" (Matt. 27:27-31).

"In this the love of God was made manifest among us, that God sent his only Son into the world, so that we might live through him" (1 John 4:9).

1. Study the passage from Matthew 27 and then list all the things Jesus suffered.
2. Why didn't Jesus stand up for His rights when He was treated unjustly?
3. Would you voluntarily go through such torture for anyone?
4. Can you think of one reason to doubt that the Jesus who went through all this for you really loves you?

Forever Love

The Bible speaks often about God's "steadfast love." Steadfast love is *forever* love. It never changes. It is always the same. Your mom might not love you for an hour after you broke her best dish. Your boyfriend or girlfriend might love you less after you disappointed him or her. Your employer may not have loved you at all the day you overslept and left the restaurant short-handed.

But God will always love you. Jesus came to earth to offer visible proof of God's eternal love. Although Jesus knew that the "rich young ruler" would not give up his wealth to follow Him, the Bible says, "And Jesus looking upon him loved him."

After Peter had denied Jesus three times, the Lord turned and looked at him. That look of love caused that tough fisherman to run out and cry. Jesus loved the woman with the bad reputation who put perfume on His feet at a dinner party, and He made her feel comfortable among the critical guests. Jesus loved Thomas the doubter and did everything possible to help him believe.

Jesus loves you and will demonstrate His love to you—if you let Him. A person can accept love only from someone he trusts. You can trust Jesus and depend on Him for never-ending love.

"The Lord is merciful and gracious, slow to anger and abounding in steadfast love. He will not always chide, nor will he keep his anger for ever. He does not deal with us according to our sins, nor requite us according to our iniquities. For as the heavens are high above the earth, so great is his steadfast love toward those who fear him. . . . As a father pities his children, so the Lord pities those who fear him. For he knows our frame; he remembers that we are dust" (Ps. 103:8-11, 13, 14).

"The steadfast love of the Lord never ceases, his mercies never come to an end" (Lam. 3:22).

1. Describe God's love.
2. Can you ever find the top of the sky? Why do you think the height of the sky ("heavens") is used in Psalm 103 to explain the extent of God's love for us?
3. Psalm 103:13, 14 are verses to read over and over again on days you can't seem to do anything right. What comfort do you find in these verses?

But You Can't Hug God!

The guy who tells a girl that he loves her and will do anything for her, and the girl who responds with the same words, make the theme for a million stories, movies, and song lyrics. Something within us longs for someone who will give himself or herself totally for us. Although we know that "and they lived happily ever after" in the children's storybooks is a myth, there's something about a total commitment to another person that we all want to experience.

The apostle Paul says that marriage is a symbol of the love between Christ and the Church. The beautiful thing is that Jesus has given himself *totally* for you. He left heaven for you. He was born in a manger for you. He put up with the Pharisees for you. He allowed Roman soldiers to put nails in His hands for you. He rose again for you. He is now in heaven praying for you.

Jesus can, and will, do everything for you. The more you think about all that Jesus has done, the more you'll want to respond to Him with a total surrender of your life. It isn't such a tough thing. It's a natural response to give to someone who has given everything for you. And even if you can't hug God, you'll discover that the relationship you can have with Him is deeper than anything you could experience with another human being.

"Blessed be the God and Father of our Lord Jesus Christ, who has blessed us in Christ with every spiritual blessing in the heavenly places, even as he chose us in him before the foundation of the world, that we should be holy and blameless before him. He destined us in love to be his sons through Jesus Christ, according to the purpose of his will, to the praise of his glorious grace which he freely bestowed on us in the Beloved" (Eph. 1:3-6).

"In this is love, not that we loved God but that he loved us and sent his Son to be the expiation (way of making amends for guilt or wrongdoing) for our sins" (1 John 4:10).

1. When did Jesus choose you?
2. Do you find it exciting that God chose you before He made the world?
3. Describe the kind of life God has planned for you.

Love Is a Two-way Street

There cannot be a relationship of love unless *both* individuals love each other and give to each other. Jesus gave himself totally to you for a great purpose: that you might surrender yourself completely to Him and enjoy His companionship.

God has enough love to satisfy you completely—even if no one else really loves you. Most people are unable to receive all of God's love because they have not given themselves totally to Him. If you really love someone, pleasing that person is more important to you than your own desires. Is pleasing Jesus the most important thing in your life? True love is very extravagant. It gives without counting the cost. Are you afraid to give up something for Jesus, or would you give up everything for Him because of all He means to you?

Several years ago, a man from India lost all he had when he became a Christian. His wife and children left him and his friends became his enemies. His comment was, "People always ask me what I gave up to become a Christian, but nobody asks me what I gained." He believed that what he had acquired was well worth the price he paid. That man knew that the more he gave in love to Jesus, the more of His love he would experience in return.

Since you're human, you may respond to God's love imperfectly, but if you daily determine to give yourself totally to God, you will have a beautiful relationship with Him.

"After these things, God tested Abraham, and said to him, 'Abraham!' And he said, 'Here am I.' He said, 'Take your son, your only son Isaac, whom you love, and go to the land of Moriah, and offer him there as a burnt offering upon one of the mountains of which I shall tell you.'

"And the angel of the Lord called to Abraham a second time from heaven, and said, 'By myself I have sworn, says the Lord, because you have done this, and have not withheld your son, your only son, I will indeed bless you . . . because you have obeyed my voice' " (Gen. 22:1-2, 15-18).

"He who has my commandments and keeps them, he it is who loves me; and he who loves me will be loved by my Father, and I will love him and manifest myself to him" (John 14:21).

1. What was the basis of the wonderful friendship Abraham had with God?

2. Do you have an "Isaac" which must be sacrificed if your relationship to God is to improve?
3. How do you think Abraham felt after he passed God's test? (Read all of Genesis 22.)

How to Get Enough Water in Your Bucket

Can you imagine a game in which the object is to get your bucket full of water by begging, borrowing, or stealing from someone else's half-full pail? Since the other players also want full buckets, the game doesn't tend to produce friendships.

Most people are playing such a game, and they are playing for keeps. Worst of all, the scarce "water" they're fighting for is *love*. Everyone needs love and tries to obtain it from other people, but people just don't have enough to give very generously. Some people completely give of themselves until they reach a certain point, and then call a sudden halt. Others give only when their love is sure to be returned. Some have been hurt and they become loners rather than risk more heartbreak. Others have no love to give and become leeches, trying to get love and attention wherever they can find it.

Obviously, what's needed is a never-ending supply of "water" from an outside source. God is a never-ending supply of love. In fact, He *is* love. He loves you now. He has loved you all your life, and will love you forever—no matter what. God can give you so much love that you can spend your life giving love to others.

"How precious is thy steadfast love, O God! The children of men take refuge in the shadow of thy wings" (Ps. 36:7).

"By day the Lord commands his steadfast love; and at night his song is with me, a prayer to the God of my life" (Ps. 42:8).

"Because thy steadfast love is better than life, my lips will praise thee" (Ps. 63:3).

"It is good to give thanks to the Lord, to sing praises to thy name, O Most High; to declare thy steadfast love in the morning, and thy faithfulness by night" (Ps. 92:1, 2).

"We love, because he first loved us" (1 John 4:19).

1. Describe God's character. (Be as specific as possible.)
2. How much time do you spend thinking and talking about God's love?

3. Think about God's love. Thank Him for being love. Memorize one of the verses.

If God Loves Me, Why Can't I Get My Locker Open?

A three-year-old's definition of love would be something like this: "If Mommy really loved me, she'd let me eat all the candy I want."

An eight-year-old's definition of love might sound like this: "If our teacher loved us, she'd let us spend four hours on the playground each day."

As we grow older our definitions don't get much better. We often feel that if God really loved us, He'd let us have our own way, give us the possessions we desire, and keep trouble away from our lives. We forget that since God *is* love, He is the One who understands love.

Love is not giving a person whatever he or she wants; God does not love you by satisfying your every whim and fancy, and you don't love others that way either. Genuine love always stays within the boundaries of God's commandments. Real love is sometimes tough—it's not always what we want. A God who really loves us will not fulfill our every desire.

We can enjoy God's love only if we accept the fact that He knows how to run His universe. If you're a cat lover, you know that some kittens can be lovingly petted on your lap and their purr will nearly drown out the TV set. With the same loving intentions, you can pick up another cat and it will spit and scratch and bristle. The difference is only a matter of the cats' attitudes. In the same way, you can choose to accept God's love or reject it. Are you a "purrer" or a "spitter"?

"Beloved, let us love one another; for love is of God, and he who loves is born of God and knows God. He who does not love does not know God; for God is love. And we have seen and testify that the Father has sent his Son as the Savior of the world. In this is love perfected with us, that we may have confidence for the day of judgment, because as he is so are we in this world. There is no fear in love, but perfect love casts out fear. For fear has to do with punishment, and he who fears is not perfected in love" (1 John 4:7, 8, 14, 17, 18).

"Keep yourselves in the love of God; wait for the mercy of our Lord Jesus Christ unto eternal life" (Jude 21).

1. According to 1 John 4, what are some signs that show God's love is in you?
2. How would you answer this question: "If God loves me, why did He allow my new ten-speed to be stolen?"
3. Have you ever been angry at God for something? Did God make a mistake or were you looking at the situation from the wrong point of view?

Nothing Else Matters

Jesus warned that if we love anyone or anything more than we love Him, we are not worthy of Him. Jesus is to be more important to us than anything else.

One can be so taken up with the beauty of the countryside that looking for landmarks or remembering the way back becomes irrelevant. Lovers can forget the time of day and even skip a meal. Have you ever loved Jesus so much that nothing else mattered or seemed the least bit important? Seeing Jesus like this will take away your sense of self-sufficiency. You will not dare to depend on yourself to serve God. The hard times that prove you are nothing in yourself will not throw you, because you realize that each time you become dependent on God in a given area, you find the real life God has for you. You will also be willing to do anything God asks—even something you would normally dislike.

Losing your life for Jesus involves giving unselfishly. I've seen a plaque which reads, "Cooking, like love, must be entered into with utter abandon, or not at all." When a person really loves someone, the gift isn't too expensive, the effort to please isn't too great, and the self-sacrifice necessary to do what the other person wants isn't too big a price to pay. Everyone else might say, "What a waste," but the person in love could care less. Do you love Jesus so much that you'll do what He wants even if everyone thinks its ridiculous?

Wholeheartedly loving Jesus means doing everything for Jesus and not for other people. If you do good deeds for the poor, help the sick, or comfort the people who hurt, you'll soon feel that these people are taking advantage of you. However, if you do all for Jesus and you love these people because Jesus loves them, it won't matter, because you're doing it only to please Jesus—and He's worth any sacrifice.

"He who loves father or mother more than me is not worthy of me; and he who loves son or daughter more than me is not worthy of me" (Matt. 10:37).

"And he [Jesus] was transfigured before them, and his face shone like the sun, and his garments became white as light. He was still speaking when lo, a bright cloud overshadowed them, and a voice from the cloud said, 'This is my beloved Son, with whom I am well pleased; listen to him.' When the disciples heard this, they fell on their faces, and were filled with awe. But Jesus came and touched them, saying, 'Rise, and have no fear.' And when they lifted up their eyes, they saw no one but Jesus only" (Matt. 17:2, 5-8).

1. Why is it logical to give all your love to Jesus?
2. Make a list of "Christian" things you do. Do you do them because you love Jesus, or for some other reason?

Week Eleven

THE RIGHT KIND OF ROMANCE

Love Is Not That Queezy Feeling in Your Stomach

After watching television or reading romantic novels, one is apt to view love as some great sensation that suddenly overwhelms a person—people fall in love while walking in the moonlight on a warm summer evening, or sitting by a fireplace after a sleigh ride, but never while cleaning the house or visiting a critically ill hospital patient. Love is generally viewed as an emotion which is either absent or present. When you ask how to recognize this unparalleled unpredictable emotion, many answer, "Don't worry, you'll just know."

Common tests for love go something like this: Do you get butterflies in your stomach every time you see that "special someone"? Do you think about this person so much you have trouble studying? Is he or she your "perfect" ideal?

Then a thousand television commercials a day declare that you must be physically attractive so that someone will be sure to fall in love with you. It would be a shame to miss it all because of using the wrong toothpaste!

But, then, people fall out of love for the most amazing reasons. Liz cut her hair, so Harry doesn't love her anymore. Jim decided to play baseball three nights a week, so Jennifer broke up with him. When Sue was asked out by a good-looking football player, she forgot all about Brian.

These misconceptions our society forces on people locks them into a treadmill of falling in and out of love, marrying, divorcing, remarrying, and divorcing. People think that if their heart skips a beat, they'd better marry the person who caused this great feeling. but as soon as the great emotional feelings leave, they get a divorce. Don't fall into that trap. It comes straight from the pit. It is not the kind of love God wants between a man and a woman.

Because this whole maze of boy-girl relationships can become such a sticky mess, you desperately need God's guidance in choosing the person to date. He or she may not even put one butterfly in your stomach—but you can count on God to give you *the very best*!

"For the Lord gives wisdom; from his mouth come knowledge and understanding. Discretion [good judgment] will watch over you; understanding will guard you" (Prov. 2:6, 11).

"Be not wise in your own eyes; fear the Lord, and turn away from evil" (Prov. 3:7).

"For the commandment is a lamp and the teaching a light, and the reproofs of discipline are the way of life, to preserve you from the evil woman, from the smooth tongue of the adventuress. Do not desire her beauty in your heart, and do not let her capture you with her eyelashes" (Prov. 6:23-25).

1. Why is "let your emotions be your guide" dangerous and unscriptural?
2. Why can God do a better job of running your dating life than you can? Are you willing to let Him control this area of your life?

Thirsty Camels and Prince Charming

The Bible defines love as an *act of the will*. It *commands* all people to love God, followers of Jesus to love their enemies, and husbands to love their wives. Because real love isn't based on emotions, a Bible love story is very different from most novels you've read. It starts with obedience to God and prayer.

Abraham obeyed God by determining not to let his son Isaac marry an idol-worshipper, even though he had to send a servant to a far country to choose a wife for his son. Imagine the faith involved in this decision! The servant prayed that God would send the right girl to the well and that she'd offer water for his camels. Sure enough, Rebekah came and offered to water his camels. When Rebekah's father and brother heard the story they answered: "The thing comes from the Lord; we cannot speak to you bad or good. Behold, Rebekah is before you, take her and go, and let her be the wife of your master's son, as the Lord has spoken" (Gen. 24:50, 51).

When they asked Rebekah if she would go to marry Isaac, she consented. It was a marriage based on God's will. Maybe that doesn't sound very romantic, but after Isaac and Rebekah had been married forty years, we read, "Abimelech king of the Philistines looked out of a window and saw Isaac fondling Rebekah his wife."

Love based solely on emotions changes if the other person does something we don't like. Love which is based first on God's will and then on our willingness to love that other person—no matter what—is the kind that lasts. That relationship will even be more romantic in the long run. Your first step toward getting in on the kind of romance God has in store is letting *God* decide whom you should or shouldn't date.

"And Isaac went out to meditate in the field in the evening; and he lifted up his eyes and looked, and behold, there were camels coming. And Rebekah lifted up her eyes, and when she saw Isaac, she alighted from the camel, and said to the servant, 'Who is the man yonder, walking in the field to meet us?' The servant said, 'It is my master.' So she took her veil and covered herself. And the servant told Isaac all the things that he had done. Then Isaac brought her into the tent, and took Rebekah and she became his wife; and he loved her. So Isaac was comforted after his mother's death" (Gen. 24:63-67).

1. What problems did Isaac and Rebekah avoid by letting God arrange their marriage?
2. What problems could you avoid by allowing God to decide whom you should date?

The True Love Exam

Skiing at top speed down your favorite slope through crisp, sparkling snow, scoring the winning touchdown in a championship game, and strolling down lovers' lane on a moonlight night can be enjoyable experiences charged with emotion. Yet, breaking a leg, dropping the ball, or starting an argument could turn these same activities into pure misery. Obviously, it's not very logical to build a life-time commitment, such as marriage, on emotions. But because emotions can be very strong and very real, it's all too easy to base everything on them.

When you're experiencing that "falling in love feeling," pray a lot. Ask God to sort out your emotions. You can *choose* to follow God no matter how you feel. Keep in mind that the Bible not only defines love as an act of the will, but also declares that love can be tested by certain attitudes found in a person. Here is the Bible's "true love exam":

"Love is patient and kind; love is not jealous or boastful; it is not arrogant or rude. Love does not insist on its own way; it is not irritable or resentful; it does not rejoice at wrong, but rejoices in the right. Love bears all things, believes all things, hopes all things, endures all things" (1 Cor. 13:4-7).

"Let love be genuine; hate what is evil, hold fast to what is good; love one another with brotherly affection; outdo one another in showing honor" (Rom. 12:9, 10).

In light of the verses you just read, check the statements that are tests of genuine love.

_____ I just *have* to be with her all the time.

_____ I'm so jealous when he pays attention to someone else.

_____ I wish he'd hurry up and get around to asking me out.

_____ When she is on vacation, I miss her so much I get crabby.

_____ He is so understanding and he is the only one who makes me feel good about myself. I just can't live without him.

_____ She'd better not be dating someone else. I wouldn't stand for it.

_____ We love each other so much we've decided to move in together.

If you checked even one of the statements, you'd better reread the verses. Every statement is *false*. The way God tests true love and the way the world tests love are very different.

Think of a guy or a girl that you are interested in. Take each quality of true love listed in the above Bible verses and write down how you could show that quality of love. (*Example*: If I really loved Jim, I'd be *patient* about his lack of organization and inability to plan ahead.)

The Bible Talks About Figs, Not Dates

"He's not a Christian but he's the nicest guy I know—a lot nicer than the *Christian* guys I know. Besides, you can't tell me what to do because *the Bible doesn't say anything about dating.*" You can't get through life without hearing that a few times. It is true that dating, as we know it, was nonexistent in Bible times, so the Bible doesn't mention it. However, this does not mean that the Bible has nothing to say on the subject.

What the Bible says about friendships and life attitudes is very applicable to dating. For example, the Bible states, "But each person is tempted when he is lured and enticed [attracted] by his own desire" (James 1:14). Dating a non-Christian automatically initiates some strong desires. You want your relationship to work out. You want to defend that person before your Christian friends. You also want to please that person and make him or her happy. Wanting very much something wrong opens the way for the devil to deceive you. You may want the person to be a Christian so badly that you convince yourself that he or she is a Christian. It's easy to close your eyes to all the faults of that person and refuse to listen to advice. If you raise an immediate defense every time someone questions your actions, you'd better talk to God and ask Him to sort out your desires.

Another thing that you do by dating a non-Christian is to encourage a false interest in the Bible or church, just to please you. The person may also be "faking it" in other areas, such as drinking and morals. If a person keeps acting a certain way just to please you, that person will begin to resent you for being his or her conscience. The only thing left will be for the two of you to break up, or for you to lower your standards. Giving God the control of your desires will keep you from hurting yourself and other people.

"Hope deferred [postponed] makes the heart sick, but a desire fulfilled is a tree of life" (Prov. 13:12).

"A desire fulfilled is sweet to the soul; but to turn away from evil is an abomination [something hateful and disgusting] to fools" (Prov. 13:19).

1. Why is dating a non-Christian, with the hope that he/she will change, so dangerous?
2. The soul is the part of you which has will, intellect, and emotions. Why do we enjoy having our desires fulfilled? What is *true* fulfillment?
3. Read Proverbs 13:19 again. Notice that even if our desires are evil, it is very hard to turn away from them. The important question is, do you really want what Jesus wants? Are there desires in your life you must give to Jesus? List them.

I Don't Need Any Advice

When your father starts out with, "When I was a boy," or, "I've lived for a long time and I know," it's easy to snap back, "But I don't need any advice!" The truth is, all of us accept advice from someone. The girl who thinks her mother's ideas are old-fashioned will constantly ask her girlfriends to help her pick out clothes; the guy who won't get a haircut to please his parents will do so immediately if he finds out his girlfriend likes short hair.

From whom will you take advice? When will you refuse to listen? These are very important decisions. The Bible says about taking advice, "A good wife is the crown of her husband, but she who brings shame is like rottenness in his bones. The thoughts of the righteous are just; the counsels [advice] of the wicked are treacherous" (Prov. 12:4, 5)

Did you notice that marrying the right person and accepting advice from the appropriate people are linked in Scripture? There are a couple of important reasons for this. First, the advice of the person you date or marry is important to you. The Bible says, "Blessed is the man who walks not in the counsel of the ungodly" (Ps. 1:1). God cannot bless you if you constantly take advice from a girlfriend or a boyfriend who is not a believer. This is one of the best reasons for deciding not to date non-Christians.

On the other hand, a person who is secure in doing the right thing listens to advice from many people without becoming defensive. The Bible teaches that we are to obey those in authority over us unless their orders are contrary to God's will. If you're constantly on the defensive and can't stand any questions from your parents, your youth director, or Christian friends about the person you date, something is wrong. Unwillingness to take advice from other Christians is very dangerous.

If you don't have Christian parents, and even if you do, find a mature Christian to advise you in your dating. Ask that person to pray for you and for your boyfriend or girlfriend. Godly advice is a valuable aid to right living.

"Where there is no guidance, a people falls; but in an abundance of counselors there is safety" (Prov. 11:14).

"By insolence [pride, disrespect for authority] the heedless make strife, but with those who take advice is wisdom" (Prov. 13:10).

"Do not be deceived: 'Bad company ruins good morals' " (1 Cor. 15:33).

1. Whose advice should you follow and whose advice should you discard?
2. What are the advantages of taking godly advice?
3. Whose advice have you been refusing that you should begin accepting?

Your Responsibility in Dating

The responsibility you have toward the person you date is the same responsibility you have toward all Christians. However, it is intensified because your relationship is so close and the opinion of the other person is so important to you. Your first responsibility is to *help the other person be the very best Christian he or she can be.* This obviously includes helping that person keep the highest moral standards. This requires some advance thinking, so when you plan a date, consider these kinds of questions: Would seeing this movie bring us closer to Christ? Would sitting around talking for a long time in the moonlight invite unnecessary temptation? Would wearing this outfit make it harder for my date to keep his thoughts pure?

Because you are Christians, your purpose in life—and on every date—is to glorify God. It is your responsibility to pray for the person you date and to encourage that person in Bible study. Be willing to give up time spent with each other so each of you can serve Christ—maybe there is a boy or girl who isn't dating who needs some of your time. Encourage the person you date to put love for Jesus above love for you. A big Scripture memorization project could be dynamite for both of you.

An important responsibility you have toward those of the opposite sex is giving them a healthy self-image. If one girl tells another she has a lousy figure, the remark, although inexcusable, can be forgotten. But if a guy says, "Well, if the fat, flat look were in, you'd make Hollywood," that girl will remember it until she's ninety.

If a girl tells a guy, "You are the clumsiest thing on two feet," that will help ruin his self-image. Flattery is wrong, but carefully worded encouragement can be invaluable in building up another Christian. Dating is a good place to practice showing consideration, kindness, and acceptance.

"How can a young man keep his way pure? By guarding it according to thy word. With my whole heart I seek thee; let me not wander from thy commandments! I have laid up thy word in my heart, that I might not sin against thee. Blessed be thou, O Lord; teach me they statutes" (Ps. 119:9-12).

"Let us then pursue what makes for peace and for mutual upbuilding" (Rom. 14:19).

1. How can you live up to the high standard of purity that God has for you?
2. After reading this passage, what place do you think studying and memorizing God's Word should have in a Christian dating relationship?
3. According to Romans 14:19, what should be your goal in a dating relationship? If you're presently in a dating relationship, are you seeking to fulfill that goal?

I'd Rather Lie Than Hurt His Feelings

After your dating relationship is ended, the person you dated will either be closer to Christ or farther away because of you. Consider that. You must be careful not to hurt the other person unnecessarily; judge your actions according to the effect they will have on him or her. Don't just consider what *you* mean but also what the other person *thinks* you mean. A popular girl has no right to flirt with a shy fellow just because she needs a New Year's Eve date, and then suddenly become "busy" for the next five months. The "goddess" who leaves a string of broken hearts behind her certainly isn't heeding Jesus' command to "love one another."

Guys, realize that girls are dreamers who make mental memory books out of all your words and actions. Don't say "I love you" unless you really mean it—she may start planning the wedding! Girls sometimes interpret an outward display of affection more deeply than was intended, so fellows need to be careful. It isn't fair to set another person up for a big let-down.

Covering up true feelings by pretending that you are going to date the person indefinitely, and then dropping him or her like a hot potato, has no place in Christian dating. If you habitually pray together, you'll find it much easier to be honest and open with each other. Besides, you need God's help. Books on marriage seem to agree that lack of communication is the number one problem in marriage. If you think being honest would ruin your relationship, it should be ruined, because it has no future.

"Put false ways far from me; and graciously teach me thy law" (Ps. 119:29)!

"Let love be genuine; hate what is evil, hold fast to what is good" (Rom. 12:9).

"Rather, speaking the truth in love, we are to grow up in every way into him who is the head, into Christ" (Eph. 4:15).

1. List some ways you could lie or create a false impression on a date.
2. In what situations is it difficult to be honest in dating?
3. Is a "but I might hurt her feelings" a good enough reason to disobey God's Word?

Week Twelve

IT'S NOT EASY TO LOVE

Broken, Bleeding Hearts and Puppy Love

"You'll get over it."

"Well, they say that puppy love is real to the puppy, but you're too young to take it so seriously."

"There are other fish in the sea."

When breaking up was not your idea, and you really hurt, none of these comments is very comforting. Although we usually associate "heartbreak" with romance, your parents' divorce, your unfulfilled dream, or moving in the middle of your senior year may be just as painful. But, there is something you can do with your broken heart. You can bring it to Jesus and He can heal it: "He heals the brokenhearted, and binds up their wounds" (Ps. 147:3).

First, confess any bitterness or resentment you feel. Bitterness and resentment are sin, and are like dirt which keeps a wound from healing unless totally cleaned out. A broken heart is bad enough. You don't need to get it full of infection.

Second, you must *want* Jesus to heal you. This may sound strange at first, but we really do enjoy self-pity. I once heard a girl admit, "Every time I talk about Bill breaking up with me, I cry, but I just love to talk about it." We all know people who fill any listening ear with all the sad tales of their lives.

Indulging in self-pity is also wrong and must be confessed. No matter how unfair the situation, no matter how much you are wronged, and no matter how deceitful the other person was, you must reject self-pity and treat it as sin.

Finally, Jesus can't heal your broken heart if you've decided that stone hearts don't hurt when they get broken—you'll just be tough and let your heart harden. Although there is always room in the "Who-Needs-Women-Anyway Gang," observe how this kind of person turns out. Because he is afraid to love and afraid to give, he keeps his distance from people. God doesn't want you to become that kind of person.

You cannot heal your own broken heart. Healing a broken heart takes a miracle—and only Jesus can do it. Be honest with Him. Tell Him the whole thing. But don't stop there. In faith, ask Him to heal your broken heart and *expect* Him to act. Hearts don't always heal instantly, so keep trusting Him, even if the hurt is still there after you've prayed. Let Jesus use the experience to draw you closer to Him.

"For he grew up before him like a young plant, and like a root out of dry ground; he had no form or comeliness that we should look at him, and no beauty that we should desire him. He was despised and rejected by men; a man of sorrows and acquainted with grief; and as one from whom men hide their faces he was despised, and we esteemed him not. Surely he has borne our griefs and carried our sorrows; yet we esteemed him stricken, smitten by God, and afflicted. But he was wounded for our transgressions, he was bruised for our iniquities; upon him was the chastisement that made us whole, and with his stripes we are healed" (Isa. 53:2-5).

1. Why is Jesus qualified to understand your heartache?
2. Do you think that Jesus's dying on the cross to make us whole and to heal us includes emotional healing? Why?

Jesus, the Heart Healer

You may feel like a Humpty Dumpty—not only all the king's horses and all the king's men, but the whole U.S. Army and all of medical science can't put you back together again. Your heart is broken into so many pieces that it's not even recognizable. The girl who is depressed because her boyfriend broke up with her might seem like "kid stuff" to you. Maybe you've used sex in the wrong way, resulting in shattering heartbreak. Maybe your home is in constant turmoil and you feel as if no one has ever cared about you. You are part of a vicious circle which goes like this: no one has really loved you, so you are afraid to or don't know how to love anyone else; therefore, no one finds you easy to love.

God's love and forgiveness offers a way out. God will forgive you and make you a new person—no matter what you've done. Receive his forgiveness and then receive His healing for your broken heart. As you give each hurt to Him, ask Jesus to heal your heartaches. Jesus can take you out of the vicious circle and put you into the winner's circle where you can receive love from God and give it to other people.

"I bless the Lord who gives me counsel; in the night also my heart instructs me. I keep the Lord always before me; because he is at my right hand, I shall not be moved. Thou dost show me the path of life; in thy presense there is fullness of joy, in thy right hand are pleasures for evermore" (Ps. 16:7, 8, 11).

"The Spirit of the Lord God is upon me, because the Lord has anointed me to bring good tidings to the afflicted; he has sent me to bind up the brokenhearted, to proclaim liberty to the captives, and the opening of the prison to those who are bound" (Isa. 61:1).

1. Reread Psalm 16:11. Where can you always find real joy in spite of what has happened to you?
2. Did Jesus heal the blind who didn't ask for help? Why not? Do you think Jesus will heal the broken hearts of people who decide to suffer through on their own or just don't bother to ask Jesus specifically for His help? Why not?

But, Everybody's Doing It!

"The only people I know of who think that sex before marriage is wrong are Queen Victoria and my grandmother." You may have heard statements like that. There's a virtual epidemic of people living together before marriage. Because the couples living together include everyone from your girlfriend's mother and her boyfriend to kids who grew up in your church, you may wonder if it can really be so bad.

When it comes to moral standards, whether or not others are doing it is *completely* irrelevant. The point is, *what does God think about it*? Older people in our country are accustomed to a society in which a majority of people supported Christian moral standards. When they were young the Christian didn't have to be "different" to have high morals. All that has changed. If you follow God's moral standards now, you are in the minority.

Although God has very important psychological and physical reasons for prohibiting sex outside of marriage, the proponents of sex before marriage can make their arguments sound very good. In this area of life as in every other, we obey what God says, because our Creator is smarter than we are, He loves us, and He knows what is best for us. What other people are doing and what may seem logical must be disregarded if it is contrary to the Bible.

If you have been involved in immorality, God offers complete forgiveness and a new life. However, there is no room in the life of a Christian for justifying sex before marriage.

"The body is not meant for immorality, but for the Lord, and the Lord for the body. Do you not know that your bodies are members of Christ? Shall I therefore take the members of Christ and make them members of a prostitute? Never! Do you not know that he who joins himself to a prostitute becomes one body with her?

For, as it is written, 'The two shall become one flesh.' But he who is united to the Lord becomes one spirit with him. Shun immorality. Every other sin which a man commits is outside the body; but the immoral man sins against his own body" (1 Cor. 6:13b, 15-18).

"For this is the will of God, your sanctification [state of being completely set apart for God, dedicated to God, holy]: that you abstain from unchastity; that each one of you know how to take a wife for himself in holiness and honor" (1 Thess. 4:3, 4).

1. Why is premarital sex wrong? List the reasons.
2. Why is the sex act meant to begin a permanent union?
3. What is God's intended purpose for our bodies?

God Lays It on the Line

If you've ever made a dress, decorated a cake, rebuilt an engine, or painted a picture, you took extremely good care of your "creation." God made you, and His rules about sex are designed to take the very best care of you. He created sex and He wants you to get the most out of it. He knows that within marriage you will receive the maximum enjoyment from sex. This does mean, of course, that you will have to give up momentary pleasure for the more lasting satisfaction. If you are given a choice between a hamburger at MacDonald's now, and a steak dinner at the best restaurant in town three hours from now, you will of course deny your stomach instant food in order to enjoy the steak. The steak dinner will taste all the better because you didn't have the hamburger.

God's rule is, "You shall not commit adultery" (Ex. 20:14). Someone has observed that God gave ten *commandments*, not ten *suggestions*! His laws are based on the fact that people have willpower and are responsible for their actions. He doesn't talk in terms of "accidents" or people who "just can't help themselves." If you have a good enough reason for not doing something, you'll refrain from it. If you knew that each action of yours would be televised on the major networks, you'd find it very possible to exercise a lot of self-control.

But you've got an even better reason for doing right: disobeying God has harsh consequences. God's rules are safeguards for us. Instead of looking on God's commandments as unwelcome restrictions, learn to say like the Psalmist, "Thy testimonies are my delight. They are my counselors" (Ps. 119:24).

"But because of the temptation to immorality, each man should have his own wife and each woman her own husband" (1 Cor. 7:2).

"Treat younger men like brothers, older women like mothers, younger women like sisters, in all purity" (1 Tim. 5:1b, 2).

"Let marriage be held in honor among all, and let the marriage bed be undefiled; for God will judge the immoral and adulterous" (Heb. 13:4).

1. How was young Timothy to treat the young women of the church?
2. Do you regard Christian young people of the opposite sex as brothers or sisters in Christ?
3. What is God's view of the position of marriage?
4. What does the Bible say about sex outside of marriage?

Are You Running a Reform School?

I was listening to "Unshackled," a Christian radio drama. The story was one of many that began with, "I married a beautiful Christian girl and she was determined to reform me, but it just didn't work out." That day I gained new insight on the issue of trying to use one's influence to reform another person.

I'd recently talked with a high school girl who was convinced she couldn't stop dating her non-Christian boyfriend because he "needed" her good influence. She had argued, "If I drop him, who will win him to Christ?"

Although I knew from experience that trying to reform any person by charm and influence was hopeless, I had never thought of it as being clearly wrong. Through that program, I saw it. Since only Jesus can redeem a soul, only Jesus can reform a life, and only He can meet every human need. When trying to help a person spiritually, any time we make that person dependent on ourselves instead of on God, we are doing something terribly wrong.

The reason that it's so easy to fall for Satan's lie at this point is that our "need to be needed" is so great. This is God's answer: In Jesus we can find everything we need so we won't need a certain person around to make us feel secure. Also, we are wanted and loved by Jesus. The poem that begins, "He has no hands but our hands to do His work today" is true. God could have been self-sufficient, but He designed the world so that He would need us to co-operate with

Him in doing His work. *That* should make you feel needed!

Also realize that if Jesus can supply our every need, He can do the same for everyone else. You can drop your non-Christian boyfriend and God will take *better care* of him than you ever could. God loves that person much more than you do. You don't have to date that good-looking non-Christian girl "just to help her," because if you really wanted to help her, you'd pray for her! There's no room for the kind of pride that says, "I can do something that God cannot do." All of us sooner or later need to realize that God is the only One who can change people from the inside out. Then we will stop trying to reform people ourselves and start praying that God will work in their lives.

"The king's heart is a stream of water in the hand of the Lord; he turns it wherever he will" (Prov. 21:2).

"O house of Israel, can I not do with you as this potter has done? says the Lord. Behold, like the clay in the potter's hand, so are you in my hand, O house of Israel" (Jer. 18:6).

1. Why isn't it your responsibility to reform anybody?
2. Are there some people you should stop trying to change and start praying for?

Love Someone You Hate

"I just can't stand that woman."

"That guy gives me the creeps."

"He'd do the human race a favor by evaporating!"

Have you ever said or thought things like that? People show great lack of love toward others for a thousand reasons: they use the wrong deoderant, they sing off-key, they talk too much, or they slurp their soup. Sometimes we try to sound "good" by saying, "I love her, but I don't like her," or, "I usually love her, but I don't today," or, "I'd love him if he'd change."

Jesus, however, commands us to love one another unconditionally—"This is my commandment, that you love one another as I have loved you" (John 15:12). Jesus loved each of us enough to die for us while we were still sinners, deserving nothing from Him. If I honestly hate Sue and God says I should love her, I can't just *say* I love her; that would make me a hypocrite. However, I can love *by faith*. I can obey God's word literally, knowing that if Jesus commanded me to love everyone, He'll give me the power to do it. I must act on that belief and love that person by faith. If I've ever done anything wrong to Sue, I apologize and make it right—even if Sue has done ten times as many bad things to me—and I don't word my apology in such a way as to expect one in return. I simply say, "Sue, I borrowed your blouse without asking you and I'm sorry. It's washed and pressed now. Will you forgive me?"

I can also do nice things for Sue, such as buy her flowers, help her with homework, and invite her to go with my friends and me to the basketball game. I don't do it by gritting my teeth and whispering under my breath, "I'm going to love Sue if it kills me," but rather, I pray, "Jesus, what I'm doing for Sue, I'm doing for you, and I'm asking you for the love I don't have." If you obey God's command to show love, sooner or later the right emotions will come tagging along behind.

"If you love those who love you, what credit is that to you? For even sinners love those who love them. And if you do good to those who do good to you, what credit is that to you? For even sinners do the same. . . . But love your enemies, and do good, and lend, expecting nothing in return; and your reward will be great, and you will be sons of the Most High; for he is kind to the ungrateful and the selfish. Be merciful, even as your Father is merciful" (Luke 6:32, 33, 35, 36).

1. Why don't we get "points" for loving people who are nice to us?
2. What reason is given for the command to love our enemies?
3. List some of the unkind and selfish people God expects you to love.
4. What's the difference between trying to love people on your own and loving them with God's love?

Love Can Melt Enemies

Maybe it's the kid at school who constantly calls you names, shoots rubber bands at you, and spreads false rumors about you; or maybe it's the person who was terribly unkind and unfair to your mother; or maybe it's the teacher who constantly scoffs at "Bible-believing fanatics"; or it could even be another Christian that you have trouble getting along with—somebody is bound to give you the opportunity to demonstrate God's dynamite weapon against enemies. *Prayer!*

God commands us to pray for our enemies. If you sincerely and constantly pray for your enemies, some exciting things will happen. For instance, you can't hate and pray at the same time. If you continue to pray, God will miraculously give you love for those who have wronged you. Also, God will work in *their* lives, and they will begin to notice that in spite of what they've done, you love them. Now, the other person will not necessarily stop hating you. In fact, he may feel so guilty that he'll treat you even worse. But God will use your actions to advertise Christianity.

If Christians don't love their enemies, they are no different from the world. God has made "love your enemies" love available to all of us. Maybe you'd better start by making a "Those Who Don't Like Me Very Much Prayer List," and pray for those people every day.

"You have heard that it was said, 'You shall love your neighbor and hate your enemy.' But I say to you, Love your enemies and pray for those who persecute you, so that you may be sons of your Father who is in heaven; for he makes his sun rise on the evil and on the good, and sends rain on the just and on the unjust. For if you love those who love you, what reward have you? Do not even the tax collectors do the same? And if you salute only your brethren, what more are you doing than others? Do not even the Gentiles do the same? You, therefore, must be perfect, as your heavenly Father is perfect" (Matt. 5:43-48).

"Repay no one evil for evil, but take thought for what is noble in the sight of all. If possible, so far as it depends on you, live peaceably with all" (Rom. 12:17, 18).

1. What are we to do for those who persecute us?
2. Is it always possible to make our enemies love us even if we love them?
3. How does God treat the people who reject Him?

THAT MOUTH OF YOURS

Does Your Tongue Need a Prison Sentence?

"Why did I say that?"

Who hasn't despairingly made that remark? All of us need discretion—the ability to say the right thing at the right time.

Living the Christian life is like operating in enemy territory—sin is everywhere and we must be on the lookout. We could make good use of armed soldiers to keep us from saying the wrong thing; and even the Psalmist said, "Set a guard over my mouth, O Lord."

And it isn't true that as long as a Christian speaks the truth, he can say anything he wishes. The person who is discreet relies on God for *every* word. This shouldn't be a self-conscious fear of opening your mouth, but the confidence a child has that he won't get lost as long as he holds his mother's hand. It's the child that goes off by himself who gets into trouble, and it's the Christian who thinks he can run his own show who falls.

There is an old saying, "What exists in the well of the thoughts will soon come up in the bucket of the speech." Guarding your speech starts with guarding your heart. Jealousy against another person can quickly cause an unkind word. Trying to protect your selfish interests can cause you to lash out at someone else. Unwillingness to see your own faults can make you defensive.

Discretion has its root in self-knowledge. We know what we're like: we're sinful and we must depend on God. Any pride or cockiness on our part means we don't know what's in the human heart. Jeremiah asks about the human heart, "Who can know it?" The answer, of course, is that only God knows, and He says it's sinful. Because we are sinful, we can't trust our own discretion, but we can exercise faith and God will give us true discretion. We best learn discretion by being silent, rather than by talking all the time. That doesn't mean you should put your tongue in jail and be afraid to say anything. Discretion balks at rashness but is quick to encourage and speak positively.

"Set a guard over my mouth, O Lord, keep watch over the door of my lips" (Ps. 141:3).

"When words are many, transgression is not lacking, but he who restrains his lips is prudent [sensible]" (Prov. 10:19).

"There is one whose rash [reckless] words are like sword thrusts, but the tongue of the wise brings healing" (Prov. 12:18).

"Be not rash with your mouth, nor let your heart be hasty to utter a word before God, for God is in heaven, and you upon earth; therefore let your words be few" (Eccles. 5:2).

1. What are the problems of talking too much?
2. How can realizing how great God is and how small you are (Eccles. 5:2) help you not to say and do rash things?
3. Have you asked God to set a guard over your lips?

Please Erase the Remark I Just Made

There's an old story about a woman who came to see her pastor. She said, "I've been guilty of spreading false rumors and now I want to undo all the damage."

The pastor told her to come with him. He bought some goose feathers and they climbed to the top of the church's bell tower. The pastor then asked the lady to drop the goose feathers. The wind quickly scattered them. "Now," the pastor ordered, "go down and gather the feathers."

"But, Pastor," protested the woman, "that would be impossible."

"I know," he replied; "just as impossible as taking back all the words you've spoken."

Words just don't disappear. You have an inner "tape deck" that keeps playing back certain words someone has said to you. Maybe it's your exasperated father roaring, "If you don't like it here, leave—and don't bother to come back!" or a teacher, at wit's end, exploding, "You're hopeless. You'll never learn algebra!"

Words like these sometimes affect us for a long time—even if the person who said them didn't really mean them. Talking is one of the most dangerous things any of us can do. Words can't be erased or obliterated, so you must think how your words will affect the other person before you say them.

People who recognize that they don't have the right to say whatever they want can get help from Jesus just by asking for it.

"I tell you, on the day of judgment men will render account for every careless word they utter" (Matt. 12:36).

"But no human being can tame the tongue—a restless evil, full of deadly poison. With it we bless the Lord and Father, and with it we curse men, who are made in the likeness of God. From the same mouth come blessing and cursing. My brethren, this ought not to be so" (James 3:8-10).

1. Who can tame the tongue?
2. What things shouldn't our tongues be used for?
3. List some specific ways in which you could be more careful about the things you say.

Your Mouth Needs a Lie Detector

A little boy once described a lie as "a terrible sin, but a very present help in time of trouble." One of the constant temptations faced by all Christians is the temptation to lie. It can be done in so many ways. "Well, it wasn't my fault," or, "What are you talking about?" slip out before we even think.

The truth, however, would sound like this: "We were playing catch too close to the window and I missed the ball"; or, "I did throw that paper airplane out the window—in fact, it was a new design"; or, "Yes, I did cheat on the test." Do you lie when you want to avoid punishment?

Then there's exaggeration—"All the other kids (all six of them) are going on the camping trip, and I'm the only one (along with four others) whose parents won't let me go"; or, "I simply must have a new dress because my old one is ragged and faded and has ink spots, glue splotches, and Dentyne on it."

Then there are lies to make us look just a little better: "I knew the answer but I just didn't say it"; "I thought the program started at 8:00 so that's why I am late"; or, "Didn't you say the theme was due on Monday instead of Friday?"

We tend to think that everybody stretches the truth a little, so it's no big deal. God thinks that lying is so bad that He included it in the Ten Commandments. You must not excuse yourself for lying, but God will forgive you if you agree with Him that lying is a sin and confess it.

Take Jesus with you through every day as your own personal Lie Detector. He will teach you how to tell the truth in every situation.

"Truthful lips endure for ever, but a lying tongue is but for a moment" (Prov. 12:19).

"Lying lips are an abomination [something hateful] to the Lord, but those who act faithfully are his delight" (Prov. 12:22).

"A righteous man hates falsehood, but a wicked man acts shamefully and disgracefully" (Prov. 13:5).

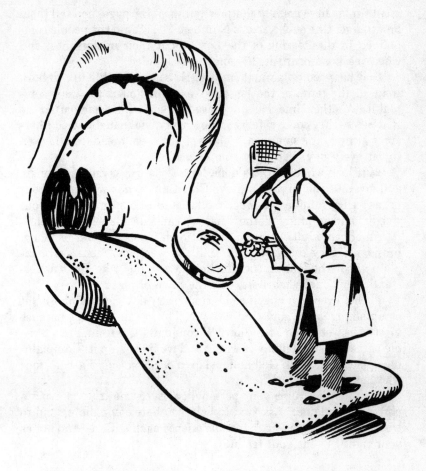

"A false witness will not go unpunished, and he who utters lies will not escape" (Prov. 19:5).

1. How does God feel about lying?
2. What will happen to liars?
3. Do you tolerate lying and do you consider "stretching" the truth as normal?

You Mean Complaining Is a Sin?

Some parts of the Old Testament are rather difficult to understand, and as you read them you think that there's nothing there that applies to you. Yet, people who keep on reading the Old Testament find many verses that almost jump off the pages and tell them how to live. One such verse is Numbers 11:1: "And the people complained in the hearing of the Lord about their misfortunes; and when the Lord heard it, his anger was kindled."

God hates complaining! In fact, He sent a terrible fire to burn some of the tents of the Israelites as punishment for their complaints. Another time, He sent poisonous snakes. He had parted the Red Sea so they could safely escape slavery, and had drowned Pharaoh's army in the same sea. He was giving them bread from heaven to eat every day. Yet, they complained.

But, look what God has done for us. He has saved us from sin and given us the Bible. We have Christian friends who care about us, as well as families, so much food that most of us must watch our weight, and so many clothes that we can't decide what to wear.

American adults complain about high taxes, the cost of living, presidents they disagree with, and the weather. Teenagers complain about the food in the lunchroom, parents' who don't understand them, mean teachers, and the price of pizza.

I'll bet even you spend some time every day complaining! But complaining is sin, and God hates it. This is hard to face because most of us would have to admit, "If complaining is a sin, I'm a terrible sinner." Complaining is wrong and we must stop it. Complaining is lack of trust in God and a slap in our Heavenly Father's face who has done so much for us.

Complaining ruins your personality. Everyone tries to avoid a chronic complainer. Ask God to help you hate complaining and to treat complaining as sin, a terrible offense against God—and not as your right to vent your feelings.

"We must not put the Lord to the test, as some of them did and were destroyed by serpents; nor grumble as some of them did and were destroyed by the Destroyer" (1 Cor. 10:9, 10).

"Do all things without grumbling or questioning, that you may be blameless and innocent, children of God without blemish in the midst of a crooked and perverse generation among whom you shine as lights in the world" (Phil. 2:14, 15).

1. What things are we warned against in these verses?
2. Pray about it and then list the specific things God would have you stop complaining about.

Snakes, Quails, and Grumblers

What we *think* affects us, but once we verbalize something, it becomes part of us in a much deeper way. People can say things so often that they end up believing them.

When I was in second grade, a boy at school started the day by saying, "I wish I could have a birthday party." By morning recess he was saying, "I'm having a birthday party," and by noon he had invited a whole group of classmates to the nonexistent party. We ran home to tell our mothers that we had been invited to a party. The boy's mother was furious.

We think we are a lot smarter than that second-grade boy—but we aren't. The grown-up Israelites in the wilderness talked so much about the "good old days" in Egypt that they forgot how cruel slavery in Egypt had been. Soon they were mad at Moses for bringing them into the terrible wilderness. It took snake bites to bring them to their senses.

Another time some Israelites started complaining that they didn't have meat to eat, and kept saying that eating manna every day was "the pits." Soon they all believed they were deprived, forsaken, and protein-starved. (They forgot that the Creator of the universe might also be a nutrition expert.) God then sent them so many quails that the greedy people got sick from eating too much.

If you keep saying something, pretty soon you'll believe it and act upon it. That means you'd better be careful what you say. Also because saying and believing the wrong thing is so serious, God must sometimes take drastic measures to keep you on track. Next time you're just about to say, "All the people at that church are hypocrites," or, "My parents don't care what I do," let visions of snakes or quails keep you from disobeying God!

"Let the words of my mouth and the meditation of my heart be acceptable in thy sight, O Lord, my rock and my redeemer" (Ps. 19:14).

"An evil man is ensnared by the transgression of his lips, but the righteous escapes from trouble" (Prov. 12:13).

"Let your speech always be gracious, seasoned with salt, so that you may know how you ought to answer every one" (Col. 4:6).

"Now may our Lord Jesus Christ himself, and God our Father, who loved us and gave us eternal comfort and good hope through grace, comfort your hearts and establish them in every good work and word" (2 Thess. 2:16, 17).

1. What are the results of saying wrong things? What happens when we say the right things?
2. God can take measures to deal with us if we speak wrongly. What will He do if we speak good things?

Did You Know That Your Mind Is on Parade?

You know the type. They have names for their teachers, such as "Skinny Neck," "Gestapo George," and "Crazy Carlson." They make nasty comments about the boy whose hair was cut too short and about the girl with the bad complexion. They constantly brag about themselves and put other people down. Their conversations are sprinkled with "I don't care what anyone says," and "Nobody is going to tell me what to do."

Such people get into arguments or fights if anyone says anything even mildly offensive to them. Listening is an activity they avoid because it would deprive them of the opportunity of loudly proclaiming what they think. When a person in authority tries to correct them, to give advice, or to ask them to follow rules laid down for everyone, they interrupt with smart remarks.

The Bible calls people like these "fools" and "scoffers"—and says some very harsh things about them. By their words they show that they are unwilling to change, or to accept correction.

How much of that description of the scoffer fits you? Someone has said, "Every time you open your mouth, your mind goes on parade." Start improving the parade by letting God deal with attitudes toward your peers, your authorities, and yourself.

"He who corrects a scoffer gets himself abuse, and he who reproves a wicked man incurs injury. Do not reprove a scoffer, or he will hate you; reprove a wise man, and he will love you. Give instruction to a wise man, and he will be still wiser; teach a righteous man, and he will increase in learning. The fear of the Lord is the beginning of wisdom, and the knowledge of the Holy One is insight" (Prov. 9:7-10).

1. What kinds of things does your speech reveal about your character?
2. How good are you at accepting correction and taking advice?
3. Where does true wisdom come from?

Oh, What a Beautiful Tongue You Have!

People often comment on beautiful eyes, flawless complexion, and lovely smiles, but no one ever says, "Oh, what a beautiful tongue you have!" Yet, that would be the nicest compliment you could ever receive—what you say can do so much good. Words of encouragement can help someone through an especially hard day. Telling your mother you love her could brighten her whole month, and saying thank you to a teacher might make him think it's been worth the effort.

Your tongue can say something cheerful when everyone else is complaining and it can say something nice about the person everyone else is putting down. The cruel things people say make living in this world extremely difficult. Your tongue can make a big difference in the atmosphere and make life easier for a lot of people.

Your tongue can also introduce people to Jesus and tell others that God loves them. Your tongue, more than any other part of your body, can make you a person worth knowing—one who brings comfort and cheerfulness wherever he goes. Stop concentrating solely on getting the world's best tan and getting your hair to go just right; start praying that God will teach you to say the right things. That's the first step toward having a beautiful tongue.

"The tongue of the wise dispenses knowledge, but the mouths of fools pour out folly" (Prov. 15:2).

"To make an apt answer is a joy to a man, and a word in season, how good it is" (Prov. 15:23).

"A word fitly spoken is like apples of gold in a setting of silver" (Prov. 25:11).

"The Lord God has given me the tongue of those who are taught, that I may know how to sustain with a word him that is weary. Morning by morning he wakens, he wakens my ear to hear as those who are taught" (Isa. 50:4).

1. Do you speak before thinking, or do you carefully decide what to say?
2. When was the last time you gave *encouragement* to someone who needed it?
3. How do we learn to say the things that would really help people? (See Isa. 50:4.)